OVERVIEW OF CONGRESSIONAL APPROPRIATIONS

CONGRESSIONAL POLICIES, PRACTICES AND PROCEDURES

Additional books in this series can be found on Nova's website under the Series tab.

Additional E-books in this series can be found on Nova's website under the E-books tab.

CONGRESSIONAL POLICIES, PRACTICES AND PROCEDURES

OVERVIEW OF CONGRESSIONAL APPROPRIATIONS

JACOB M. STEWART
AND
DANIELLE M. ALLWORTH
EDITORS

Nova Science Publishers, Inc.
New York

Library of Congress Cataloging-in-Publication Data

Overview of congressional appropriations / editors, Jacob M. Stewart and Danielle M. Allworth.
    p. cm.
  Includes index.
  ISBN 978-1-61209-849-4 (hardcover)
  1. United States--Appropriations and expenditures. 2. United States. Congress--Appropriations and expenditures. 3. Budget process--United States. I. Stewart, Jacob M. II. Allworth, Danielle M.
  HJ2051.O94 2011
  328.73'0778--dc22
                        2011004610

Published by Nova Science Publishers, Inc. † New York

CONTENTS

Preface   **vii**

Chapter 1   The Congressional Appropriations Process:
                An Introduction   **1**
                Sandy Streeter

Chapter 2   Advance Appropriations, Forward Funding,
                and Advance Funding   **33**
                Sandy Streeter

Chapter 3   Omnibus Appropriations Acts:
                Overview of Recent Practices   **37**
                Jessica Tollestrup

Chapter 4   Annual Appropriations Acts: Consideration
                during Lame-Duck Sessions   **55**
                Jessica Tollestrup

Chapter 5   House Offset Amendments to Appropriations
                Bills: Procedural Considerations   **75**
                Sandy Streeter

Chapter 6   Legislative Branch Appropriations Bill:
                Structure, Content, and Process   **95**
                Lorraine H. Tong

Chapter 7   Examples of Legislative Provisions
                in Annual Appropriations Act   **101**
                Robert Keith

Chapter 8   Supplemental Appropriations: Trends
                  And Budgetary Impacts Since 1981   **125**
                  Thomas L. Hungerford

Chapter 9   State, Foreign Operations Appropriations:
                  A Guide to Component Accounts   **137**
                  Curt Tarnoff and Kennon H. Nakamura

Chapter Sources   **157**

Index   **159**

PREFACE

This new book provides an overview of congressional appropriations; forward funding and advance funding; omnibus appropriations and house offset amendments.

Chapter 1- Congress annually considers several appropriations measures, which provide funding for numerous activities, for example, national defense, education, and homeland security, as well as general government operations. Congress has developed certain rules and practices for the consideration of appropriations measures, referred to as the *congressional appropriations process*.

Chapter 2- Apppropriations acts generally make budget authority (or BA) available for use (or obligation) at the start of the fiscal year covered by the act. For example, the FY2010 appropriations acts generally made budget authority available on October 1, 2009. Sometimes appropriations bills provide a different date for specified budget authority within the act to become first available so that the funding cycle does not coincide with the fiscal year generally covered by the act. There are three types of this kind of budget authority: advance appropriations, forward funding, and advance funding.

Chapter 3 - Omnibus appropriations acts have become a significant feature of the legislative process in recent years as Congress and the President have used them more frequently to bring action on the regular appropriations cycle to a close. Following a discussion of pertinent background information, this report reviews the recent enactment of such measures and briefly addresses several issues raised by their use.

Chapter 4- Seven of the past eight Congresses, covering the 103rd Congress through the 110th Congress, have concluded with a lame-duck session (no such session occurred in 1996, during the 104th Congress). The consideration of annual appropriations acts has been an important element of some, but not all, of these lame-duck sessions. Although no annual appropriation acts were considered during lame-duck sessions held in 1994, 1998, and 2008, a total of 14 regular and 11 continuing appropriations acts were considered and subsequently enacted into law during the four other lame-duck sessions held in 2000, 2002, 2004, and 2006.

Chapter 5- One of the most common methods for changing spending priorities in appropriations bills on the House floor is through *offset amendments*. House offset amendments generally change spending priorities in a pending appropriations measure by increasing spending for certain activities (or creating spending for new activities not included in the bill) and offsetting the increase with funding decreases in other activities in the bill. Offset amendments are needed to avoid the Congressional Budget Act 302(f) and 311(a) points of order enforcing certain spending ceilings.

Chapter 6- The legislative branch appropriations bill is one of the regular appropriations bills that Congress considers each year. It provides budget authority to spend specified amounts of money for expenditures of the legislative branch for the fiscal year, including staff salaries. This bill funds the operations not only of Congress itself but also of its support agencies and other entities within the legislative branch. Salaries for Members of Congress are not included in the annual bill, but are funded automatically each year in a permanent appropriations account.

Chapter 7- Over the years, House and Senate rules generally have been used to promote the separate consideration of substantive legislation and measures providing annual appropriations to federal agencies, chiefly so that the regular funding of the federal government is not impeded by controversies associated with authorizing and other legislation.

Chapter 8- Hurricane Katrina, which struck Louisiana, Mississippi, and Alabama in 2005, caused widespread flooding, significant property damage, and lost lives. Within two weeks, Congress passed two supplemental appropriations measures providing a combined $62.3 billion for relief and recovery needs. Including the supplementals for the war on terror and military operations in Iraq and Afghanistan, total supplemental appropriations for FY2005 to FY2008 were $512.7 billion. In response, there is growing sentiment in Congress that military operations be funded through the regular appropriations process rather than through supplemental appropriations.

Chapter 9- The State, Foreign Operations, and Related Programs appropriations legislation provides annual funding for almost all of the international affairs programs generally considered as part of the 150

International Affairs Budget Function (the major exception being food assistance). In recent years, the legislation has also served as a vehicle for Congress to place conditions on the expenditure of those funds, and express its views regarding certain foreign policy issues.

In: Overview of Congressional Appropriations   ISBN: 978-1-61209-849-4
Editors: J.M. Stewart, D.M. Allworth   © 2011 Nova Science Publishers, Inc.

Chapter 1

THE CONGRESSIONAL APPROPRIATIONS PROCESS: AN INTRODUCTION

Sandy Streeter

SUMMARY

Congress annually considers several appropriations measures, which provide funding for numerous activities, for example, national defense, education, and homeland security, as well as general government operations. Congress has developed certain rules and practices for the consideration of appropriations measures, referred to as the *congressional appropriations process*.

Appropriations measures are under the jurisdiction of the House and Senate Appropriations Committees. In recent years these measures have provided approximately 35% of total federal spending. The remainder of federal spending comprises direct (or mandatory) spending controlled by House and Senate legislative committees and net interest on the public debt.

There are three types of appropriations measures. *Regular appropriations bills* provide most of the funding that is provided in all appropriations measures for a fiscal year, and must be enacted by October 1, the beginning of the fiscal year. If regular bills are not enacted by the beginning of the new fiscal year, Congress adopts *continuing resolutions* to continue funding, generally until regular bills are enacted. *Supplemental appropriations bills* provide additional appropriations to become available during a fiscal year.

Each year Congress considers a budget resolution that, in part, sets spending ceilings for the upcoming fiscal year. Both the House and Senate have established parliamentary rules that enforce certain spending ceilings associated with the budget resolution during consideration of appropriations measures in the House and Senate, respectively.

Congress has also established an authorization-appropriation process that provides for two separate types of measures—authorization bills and appropriation bills. These measures perform different functions. Authorization bills establish, continue, or modify agencies or programs. Appropriations measures subsequently provide funding for the agencies and programs authorized.

INTRODUCTION

Congress annually considers several appropriations measures, which provide funding for numerous activities, such as national defense, education, and homeland security, as well as general government operations. These measures are considered by Congress under certain rules and practices, referred to as the *congressional appropriations process*. This report discusses the following aspects of this process:

- the annual appropriations cycle;
- types of appropriations measures;
- spending ceilings for appropriations associated with the annual budget resolution; and
- the relationship between authorization and appropriation measures.

When considering appropriations measures, Congress is exercising the power granted to it under the Constitution, which states, "No money shall be drawn from the Treasury, but in Consequence of Appropriations made by Law."[1] The power to appropriate is a legislative power. Congress has enforced its prerogatives through certain laws. The so-called Antideficiency Act, for example, strengthened the application of this section by, in part, explicitly prohibiting federal government employees and officers from making contracts or other obligations in advance of or in excess of an appropriation, unless authorized by law; and providing administrative and criminal sanctions for those who violate the act.[2] Under law, public funds, furthermore, may only be used for the purpose(s) for which Congress appropriated the funds.[3]

The President has an important role in the appropriations process by virtue of his constitutional power to approve or veto entire measures, which Congress can only override by two-thirds vote of both chambers. He also has influence, in part, because of various duties imposed by statute, such as submitting an annual budget to Congress.

The House and Senate Committees on Appropriations have jurisdiction over the annual appropriations measures. Each committee has 12 subcommittees and each subcommittee has jurisdiction over one regular annual appropriations bill that provides funding for departments and agencies under the subcommittee's jurisdiction.[4]

The jurisdictions of the House and Senate appropriations subcommittees are generally parallel. That is, each House appropriations subcommittee is paired with a Senate appropriations subcommittee and the two subcommittees' jurisdictions are generally identical.[5] As currently organized, there are 12 subcommittees:[6]

- Agriculture, Rural Development, Food and Drug Administration, and Related Agencies (Agriculture);
- Commerce, Justice, Science, and Related Agencies (Commerce, Justice, and Science);
- Defense;
- Energy and Water Development, and Related Agencies (Energy and Water Development);
- Financial Services and General Government;
- Homeland Security;
- Interior, Environment, and Related Agencies (Interior and Environment);
- Labor, Health and Human Services, Education, and Related Agencies (Labor, Health and Human Services, and Education);
- Legislative Branch;
- Military Construction, Veterans Affairs, and Related Agencies (Military Construction and Veterans Affairs);
- State, Foreign Operations, and Related Programs (State and Foreign Operations); and
- Transportation, and Housing and Urban Development, and Related Agencies (Transportation and Housing and Urban Development).

ANNUAL APPROPRIATIONS CYCLE

President Submits Budget

The President initiates the annual budget cycle when he submits his annual budget for the upcoming fiscal year[7] to Congress. He is required to submit his annual budget on or before the first Monday in February.[8] Congress has, however, provided deadline extensions; both statutorily and, sometimes, informally.[9]

The President recommends spending levels for various programs and agencies of the federal government in the form of *budget authority* (or *BA*). Such authority does not represent cash provided to, or reserved for, agencies. Instead, the term refers to authority provided by federal law to enter into contracts or other financial *obligations* that will result in immediate or future expenditures (or *outlays*) involving federal government funds. Most appropriations are a form of budget authority that also provide legal authority to make the subsequent payments from the Treasury.

An FY2010 appropriations act, for example, provided $79 million in new budget authority for FY2010 to the National Institute of Environmental Health Sciences for agency operations.[10] That is, the act gave the Institute legal authority to sign contracts to purchase supplies and pay salaries. The agency could not commit the government to pay more than $79 million for these covered activities. The outlays occur when government payments are made to complete the tasks.

While budget authority must be obligated in the fiscal year(s) in which the funds are made available, outlays may occur over time. In the case of the Institute's activities, it may not pay for all the supplies until the following fiscal year.

The amount of outlays in a fiscal year may vary among activities funded because the length of time to complete the activities differs. Outlays to pay salaries may occur in the year the budget authority is made available, while outlays for a construction project may occur over several years as various stages of the project are completed.

As Congress considers appropriations measures providing new budget authority for a particular fiscal year, discussions on the resulting outlays involve estimates based on historical trends. Data on the actual outlays for a fiscal year are not available until the fiscal year has ended.

After the President submits his budget to Congress, each agency generally provides additional detailed *justification* materials to the House and Senate appropriations subcommittees with jurisdiction over its funding.

Congress Adopts Budget Resolution

The Congressional Budget and Impoundment Control Act of 1974 (Congressional Budget Act)[11] requires Congress to adopt an annual budget resolution. [12] The budget resolution is Congress's response to the President's budget. The budget resolution must cover at least five fiscal years: the upcoming fiscal year plus the four subsequent fiscal years.

The budget resolution, in part, sets total new budget authority and outlay levels for each fiscal year covered by the resolution. It also allocates federal spending among generally 20 functional categories (such as national defense, agriculture, and transportation) and sets similar levels for each function.

Within each chamber, the total new budget authority and outlays for each fiscal year are also allocated among committees with jurisdiction over spending, thereby setting spending ceilings for each committee (see "Allocations" section below). [13] The House and Senate Committees on Appropriations receive allocations only for the upcoming fiscal year, because appropriations measures are annual. Once the appropriations committees receive their spending ceilings, they separately subdivide the amount among their respective subcommittees, providing spending ceilings for each subcommittee.[14]

The budget resolution is not sent to the President, and does not become law. It does not provide budget authority or raise or lower revenues; instead, it is a guide for the House and Senate as they consider various budget-related bills, including appropriations and tax measures. Both the House and Senate have established parliamentary rules to enforce some of these spending ceilings when legislation is considered on the House or Senate floor, respectively.[15]

The Congressional Budget Act establishes April 15 as a target for congressional adoption of the budget resolution. During the past 34 fiscal years Congress has considered budget resolutions (FY1 977-FY20 10), however, Congress frequently has not met this target, and in four of those years (FY1999, FY2003, FY2005, and FY2007), Congress did not adopt a budget resolution.[16]

There is no penalty if the budget resolution is not completed before April 15, or not at all. Under the Congressional Budget Act, however, certain enforceable spending ceilings associated with the budget resolution are not established until the budget resolution is completed. The act also prohibits both House and Senate floor consideration of appropriations measures for the upcoming fiscal year before they complete the budget resolution; and, in the Senate, before the Senate Appropriations Committee receives its spending ceilings.[17] The House, however, may consider most appropriations measures after May 15, even if the budget resolution is not in place;[18] and the Senate may adopt a motion to waive this rule by a majority vote.

If Congress delays completion of the annual budget resolution (or does not adopt one), each chamber may adopt a deeming resolution to address these procedural difficulties.[19]

Timetable for Consideration of Appropriations Measures

It is important to note that the timing of the various stages of the appropriations process tends to vary from year to year. While timing patterns for each stage tend to be discernible over time, certain anomalies from these general patterns occur in many years.

Traditionally, the House of Representatives initiated consideration of regular appropriations measures, and the Senate subsequently considered and amended the House-passed bills. Recently, the Senate appropriations subcommittees and committee have sometimes not waited for the House bills, instead it has reported original Senate bills. Under this non-traditional approach, the House and Senate appropriations committees and their subcommittees have often considered the regular bills simultaneously.

The House Appropriations Committee reports the 12 regular appropriations bills separately to the full House.[20] The committee generally begins reporting the bills in May or June, typically completing their consideration of all of them prior to the annual August recess.[21] Generally, the full House starts consideration of the regular appropriations bills in May or June as well, passing almost all of them by the August recess.[22] The regular bills that do not pass are typically funded in an omnibus appropriations bill.[23]

In the Senate, the Senate Appropriations Committee typically begins reporting the bills in June and generally completes committee consideration in September.[24] The Senate typically passes the bills in June or July and continues through the fall. For four of the past eight fiscal years (FY2004-FY20 11), the Senate also did not pass a majority of the bills.[25]

During the fall and winter, the appropriations committees are usually heavily involved in negotiations to resolve differences between the versions of appropriations bills passed by their respective chambers. Relatively little (if any) time is left before the fiscal year begins to resolve what may be wide disparities between the House and Senate, to say nothing of those between Congress and the President. As a result, Congress is usually faced with the need to enact one or more temporary continuing resolutions pending the final disposition of the regular appropriations bills.[26]

In four of the past seven fiscal years (FY2004-FY20 1 0),[27] all of the regular bills (either separately or in omnibus bills) became law by the end of the calendar year. In three years, they were completed early in the following calendar year.

Work of the Appropriations Committees

After the President submits his budget, the House and Senate appropriations subcommittees hold hearings on the segments of the budget under their jurisdiction. They focus on the details of the agencies' justifications, primarily obtaining testimony from agency officials.

After the hearings have been completed, and the House and Senate Appropriations Committees have generally received their spending ceilings, the subcommittees begin to mark up[28] the regular bills under their jurisdiction and report them to their respective full committees. (Each year a few Senate appropriations subcommittees do not formally report the regular bill to the full committee; in such cases, formal committee action begins at full-committee markup.) Both Appropriations Committees consider each subcommittee's recommendations separately. The committees may adopt amendments to a subcommittee's recommendations, and then report the bill as amended to their respective floors for further action.

House and Senate Floor Action

After the House or Senate Appropriations Committee reports an appropriations bill to the House or Senate, respectively, the bill is available on the floor. At this point, Representatives or Senators are generally provided an opportunity to propose floor amendments to the bill.

House

Prior to floor consideration of a regular appropriations bill, the House generally considers a special rule reported by the House Committee on Rules setting parameters for floor consideration of the bill.[29] If the House adopts the special rule, it usually considers the appropriations bill immediately.

The House considers the bill in the Committee of the Whole House on the State of the Union (or Committee of the Whole) of which all Representatives are members.[30] A special rule on an appropriations bill usually provides for one hour of general debate on the bill. The debate includes opening statements by the chair and ranking minority member[31] of the appropriations subcommittee with jurisdiction over the regular bill, as well as other interested Representatives.

After the Committee of the Whole debates the bill, it considers amendments. A regular appropriations bill is generally read for amendment, by paragraph.[32] Amendments must meet a variety of requirements:

- House standing rules and precedents generally that establish several requirements, such as requiring amendments to be germane to the bill;
- House standing rules and precedents that establish a separation between legislation and appropriations (see "Relationship Between Authorization and Appropriation Measures" below);
- funding limits imposed by the congressional budget process (see "Spending Ceilings for Appropriations Measures" below); and
- provisions of a special rule or unanimous consent agreement providing for consideration of the particular bill.

If an amendment violates any of these requirements, any Representative may raise a point of order to that effect. If the presiding officer rules the amendment out of order, it cannot be considered on the House floor. The special rule or unanimous consent agreement[33] may waive the requirements imposed by House rules or the budget process, thereby allowing the House to consider the amendment.

During consideration of individual regular appropriations bills, the House sometimes sets additional parameters, either by adopting a special rule or by unanimous consent. For example, the House sometimes agrees to limit consideration to a specific list of amendments or to limit debate on individual amendments by unanimous consent.

After the Committee of the Whole completes consideration of the measure, it rises and reports the bill and any amendments that have been adopted to the full House. The House then votes on the amendments and passage. After House passage, the bill is sent to the Senate.

Senate

The full Senate considers the bill as reported by its appropriations committee.[34] The Senate does not have a device like a special rule to set parameters for consideration of bills. Before taking up the bill, however, or during its consideration, the Senate sometimes sets parameters by unanimous consent.

When the bill is brought up on the floor, the chair and ranking minority member of the appropriations subcommittee make opening statements on the contents of the bill as reported. Committee and floor amendments to the reported bills must meet requirements established under the Senate standing rules and precedents (including those providing for the separation of authorizations and appropriations) and congressional budget process, as well as requirements agreed to by unanimous consent. The specifics of the Senate and House requirements differ, including the waiver procedures.[35]

The Senate, in contrast to the House, does not consider floor amendments in the order of the bill. Senators may propose amendments to any portion of the bill at any time unless the Senate agrees to set limits.

House and Senate Conference Action

Generally, members of the House and Senate appropriations subcommittees having jurisdiction over a particular regular appropriations bill, and the chair and ranking minority members of the full committees meet to negotiate over differences between the House- and Senate-passed bills.[36]

Under House and Senate rules, the negotiators (called *conferees* or *managers*) are generally required to remain within the scope of the differences between the positions of the two chambers, and cannot add new matter.[37] Their agreement must be within the range established by the House- and Senate-passed versions. For example, if the House-passed bill appropriates $3 million for a program and a separate Senate amendment provides $5 million, the conferees must reach an agreement that is within the $3 million-$5 million range. In the Senate, the conference report cannot add new directed spending provisions that were not in included in either the House- or Senate-passed versions of the bill. The Senate rule against new matter applies to any provision in the conference report, while the rule against new directed spending provisions is limited to

> any item that consists of a specific provision containing a specific level of funding for any specific account, specific program, specific project, or specific activity, when no specific funding was provided for such specific account, specific program, specific project, or specific activity in the measure originally committed to the conferees by either House.[38]

These rules may be enforced during House and Senate consideration of the conference report.

In current practice the Senate typically passes the House bill with the Senate version attached as a single substitute amendment. In such instances, the conferees must reach agreement on all points of difference between the House and Senate versions before reporting the conference report to both houses. When this occurs, the conferees propose a new conference substitute for the bill as a whole. The conference report includes a *joint explanatory statement* (or *managers' statement*) explaining the new substitute. A conference report may not be amended in either chamber.

Usually, the House considers conference reports on appropriations measures first, because it traditionally considers the measures first. Prior to consideration of the conference report, the House typically adopts a special rule waiving any points of order against the conference report. The first chamber to consider the conference report has the option of voting to recommit it to the conference for further consideration, rejecting it, or adopting it.

After the first house adopts the conference report, the conference is automatically disbanded; therefore, the second house has two options—adopt or reject the conference report. The Senate, however, may strike new matter or new directed spending provisions from the conference report by points of order thereby rejecting it. The Senate can avoid this situation by adopting a motion to waive the applicable rule by a three-fifths vote of all Senators duly chosen and sworn (60 Senators if there are no vacancies). If the Presiding Officer sustains point(s) of order against new matter or new directed spending provisions, the offending language is stricken from the conference report. After all points of order under both requirements have been disposed of, the

Senate considers a motion to send the remaining provisions to the House as an amendment between the houses since they cannot amend the conference report. The House would then consider the amendment. The House may choose to further amend the Senate amendment and return to the Senate for further consideration. If the House, however, agrees to the amendment the measure is sent to the President.[39]

In cases in which either the conference report is rejected or recommitted to the conference committee, the conferees negotiate further over the matters in dispute between the two houses.[40] The measure cannot be sent to the President until both houses have agreed to the entire text of the bill.

Presidential Action

Under the Constitution,[41] after Congress sends the bill to the President, he has 10 days to sign or veto the measure. If he takes no action, the bill automatically becomes law at the end of the 10- day period. Conversely, if he takes no action when Congress has adjourned, he may *pocket veto* the bill.

If the President vetoes the bill, he sends it back to Congress. Congress may override the veto by a two-thirds vote in both houses. If Congress successfully overrides the veto, the bill becomes law. If Congress is unsuccessful, the bill dies.

TYPES OF APPROPRIATIONS MEASURES

There are three major types appropriations measures: regular appropriations bills, continuing resolutions, and supplemental appropriations measures. Of the three types, regular appropriations bills typically provide most of the funding.[42]

Regular Appropriations Bills

The House and Senate annually consider 12 regular appropriations measures. Each House and Senate appropriations subcommittee has jurisdiction over one regular bill.

Regular appropriations bills contain a series of unnumbered paragraphs with headings; generally reflecting a unique budget account. The basic unit of regular and supplemental appropriations bills is the account. Under these measures, funding for each department and large independent agency is distributed among several accounts. Each account, generally, includes similar programs, projects, or items, such as a research and development account or salaries and expenses account. For small agencies, a single account may fund all of the agency's activities. These acts typically provide a lump-sum amount for each account as well as any conditions, provisos, or specific requirements that apply to that account. A few accounts include a single program, project, or item, which the appropriations act funds individually.

In report language,[43] the House and Senate Committees on Appropriations provide more detailed directions to the departments and agencies on the distribution of funding among various activities funded within an account. Congressional earmarks (referred to as congressionally directed spending items in Senate Rule XLIV) are frequently included in report language and have also been provided in bills, amendments, or conference reports.

Appropriations measures may also provide transfer authority.[44] *Transfers* shift budget authority from one account or fund to another. For example, an agency moving new budget authority from a salaries and expenses account to a research and development account would be a transfer. Agencies are prohibited from making such transfers without statutory authority.

In contrast, agencies may generally shift budget authority from one activity to another within an account without such statutory authority. This is referred to as *reprogramming*.[45] The appropriations subcommittees have established notification and other oversight procedures for the various agencies to follow regarding reprogramming actions. Generally, these procedures differ with each subcommittee.

Congress has traditionally considered and approved each regular appropriations bill separately, but Congress has also combined several bills together. For 21 of the past 34 years (FY1 977- FY20 10), Congress has packaged two or more regular appropriations bills together in one measure.[46] These packages are referred to as omnibus appropriation measures.[47]

In these cases, Congress typically began consideration of each regular bill separately, but generally has combined some of the bills together at the conference stage. During conference on a single regular appropriations bill, the conferees typically have included in the conference report the final agreements on other outstanding regular appropriations bills, thereby creating an omnibus appropriations measure.[48]

During the past 34 years, omnibus measures have been used during two time periods: a nine-year period (FY1980-FY1988) and a 15-year period (FY1996-FY2010), as shown in Table 1. During the first period, packaging was used for nine consecutive fiscal years. The first two of those years (FY1 980-FY1 981) occurred while President Jimmy Carter was in the White House, and the remaining seven were during Ronald Reagan's presidency. In the last 15 years (FY1995-FY20 10), omnibus measures were enacted for 12 years—five during President William Jefferson Clinton's presidency (FY1996-FY1997 and FY1999-FY2001), six during President George W. Bush presidency (FY2003-FY2005 and FY2007-FY2009), and one while President Barack H. Obama has been in the White House (FY20 10).[49]

All the regular appropriations bills for a given fiscal year were included in omnibus measures for three of the past 34 years. In two years (FY1987 and FY1988), all of the bills were enacted in a single omnibus bill; and for FY2009, all the bills were packaged, but in two separate measures. Three FY2009 regular bills were included in single omnibus act, while the remaining nine bills were packaged in another omnibus bill.

Packaging regular appropriations bills can be an efficient means for resolving outstanding differences within Congress or between Congress and the President. The negotiators can make more convenient trade-offs between issues among several bills and complete consideration of appropriations using fewer measures.

Table 1. Number of Regular Appropriations Bills Packaged in Omnibus (or Minibus) Measure, FY1 977-FY20 10

Fiscal Year	Presidential Administration	Regular Acts in Omnibus or Minibus Measure
1977	Gerald Ford	0
1978	Jimmy Carter	0
1979		0
1980		2
1981		5
1982	Ronald Reagan	3
1983		6
1984		3
1985		8
1986		7
1987		13

Table 1. (Continued)

Fiscal Year	Presidential Administration	Regular Acts in Omnibus or Minibus Measure
1988		13
1989		0
1990	George H.W. Bush	0
1991		0
1992		0
1993		0
1994	William Clinton	0
1995		0
1996		5
1997		6
1998		0
1999		8
2000		5
2001		2,3a
2002	George W. Bush	0
2003		11
2004		7
2005		9
2006		0
2007		9
2008		11
2009		3,9b
2010	Barack H. Obama	6

Sources: U.S. Congress, Senate Committee on Appropriations, *Appropriations, Budget Estimates, Etc.*, committee prints, 94th Cong., [2nd] sess.- 103rd , Cong., [2nd] sess. (Washington: GPO, 1976-1994); and U.S. Congress, House, *Calendars of the U.S. House of Representatives and History of Legislation, 94th-111th Congresses* (Washington: GPO, 1976- 2009).

a. The FY2001 Energy and Water Development bill was attached to the FY2001 Veterans Affairs, Housing and Urban Development, and Independent Agencies act (P.L. 106-377, 114 Stat. 1441). The FY2001 Legislative Branch bill and Treasury and General Government bill were attached to the FY2001 Labor, Health and Human Services, Education, and Related Agencies act (P.L. 106-554, 114 Stat. 2763).

b. The FY2009 Defense, Homeland Security, and Military Construction-VA regular appropriations bills were included in a separate bill, Consolidated Security, Disaster Assistance, and Continuing Appropriations Act, 2009 (P.L. 110-329, 122 Stat. 3574); and the remaining nine regular bills were included in another separate act, Omnibus Appropriations Act, 2009 (P.L. 111-8, 123 Stat. 524).

Continuing Resolutions

The provisions in regular appropriations bills typically allow funds to be obligated only until the end of the fiscal year, October 1. If action on one or more regular appropriations measures has not been completed by that date, the agencies funded by these bills must cease nonessential activities due to lack of budget authority. Traditionally, *continuing appropriations* have been used to maintain temporary funding for agencies and programs until the regular bills are enacted. Such appropriations continuing funding are usually provided in a joint resolution, hence the term *continuing resolution* (or *CR*).

In 29 of the past 34 years (FY1 977-FY20 10), Congress and the President did not complete action on a majority of the regular bills prior to the start of the fiscal year (see **Table 2**). In nine years, they did not finish any of the bills before October 1. They completed action on all the bills on schedule only four times: FY1977, FY1989, FY1995, and FY1997.

On or before the start of the fiscal year, Congress and the President generally complete action on an initial continuing resolution that temporarily funds the outstanding regular appropriations bills. In contrast to funding practices in regular bills (i.e., providing appropriations for each account), temporary continuing resolutions generally provide funding by a rate and/or formula. Recently, the continuing resolutions have generally provided a rate at the levels provided in the previous fiscal year. The initial CR typically provides temporary funding until a specific date or until the enactment of the applicable regular appropriations acts, if earlier. Once the initial CR becomes law, additional interim continuing resolutions are frequently used to sequentially extend the expiration date. These subsequent continuing resolutions sometimes change the funding methods. Over the past 33 fiscal years (FY1978-FY2010), Congress has approved, on average, four continuing resolutions each year (see **Table 2**).

Supplemental Appropriations Measures

Congress frequently considers one or more supplemental appropriations measures (or supplementals) for a fiscal year that generally increase funding for selected activities previously funded in the regular bills. Recent supplementals have also been used to provide funds for the wars in Iraq and Afghanistan. Supplementals may provide funding for unforeseen needs (such as funds to recover from a hurricane, earthquake or flood); or increase or provide funding for other activities. These measures, like regular appropriations bills, provide specific amounts of funding for individual accounts in the bill. Sometimes Congress includes supplemental appropriations in regular bills and continuing resolutions rather than in a separate supplemental bill.

Table 2. Regular Appropriations Bills Completed by Deadline and Number of Continuing Resolutions, FY1 977-FY2010

Fiscal Year	Presidential Administration	Regular Appropriations Bills Became Law by or on October 1st	Continuing Resolutions Became Law
1977	Gerald Ford	13	(2ᵃ)
1978	Jimmy Carter	9	3
1979		5	1
1980		3	2
1981		1	3
1982	Ronald Reagan	0	4
1983		1	2
1984		4	2
1985		4	5
1986		0	5
1987		0	5
1988		0	5
1989		13	0
1990	George H.W. Bush	1	3
1991		0	5
1992		3	4
1993		1	1
1994	William J. Clinton	2	3
1995		13	0
1996		0	13
1997		13ᵇ	0
1998		1	6
1999		1	6
2000		4	7
2001		2	21
2002	George W. Bush	0	8

Table 2. (Continued)

Fiscal Year	Presidential Administration	Regular Appropriations Bills Became Law by or on October 1st	Continuing Resolutions Became Law
2003		0	8
2004		3	5
2005		1	3
2006		2	3
2007		1	4[c]
2008		0	4[d]
2009		3[e]	2[f]
2010	Barack H. Obama	1	2[g]

Sources: U.S. Congress, Senate Committee on Appropriations, *Appropriations, Budget Estimates, Etc.*, 94th Cong., 2nd sess.- 104th Cong., [1st] sess. (Washington: GPO, 1976-1995). U.S. Congress, House, *Calendars of the U.S. House of Representatives and History of Legislation*, 104th Cong., [1st] sess.- 111th Cong., [1st] sess. (Washington: GPO, 1995-2009).

a. The two CRs did not provide continuing funding for entire regular bills; instead, they provided funding for selected activities.

b. Five regular bills were attached to the FY1997 defense regular act (P.L. 104-208, 110 Stat. 3009), which became law on September 30. As a result, the FY1997 appropriations process was completed by October 1.

c. Initial FY2007 continuing appropriations were included, as Division B, in the FY2007 Defense regular appropriations act (P.L. 109-289, 120 Stat. 1257, 1311).

d. Continuing appropriations that extended the initial FY2008 continuing resolution were included, as Division B, in the FY2008 Defense regular appropriations act (P.L. 110-116, 121 Stat. 1295, 1341).

e. Three FY2009 regular appropriations bills were included in an FY2009 omnibus measure, Consolidated Security, Disaster Assistance, and Continuing Appropriations Act, 2009, that became law on September 30, 2008 (P.L. 110-329, 122 Stat. 3574). Initial FY2009 continuing appropriations and certain FY2008 supplemental appropriations were also included in this act.

f. Initial FY2009 continuing appropriations were included, as Division A, in a three-bill FY2009 omnibus act, Consolidated Security, Disaster Assistance, and Continuing Appropriations Act, 2009 (P.L. 110-329, 122 Stat. 3574).

g. Initial FY20 10 continuing appropriations were included, as Division B, in the FY20 10 Legislative Branch regular appropriations bill (P.L. 111-68, 123 Stat. 2023, 2043). Final FY20 10 continuing appropriations were included, as Division B, in FY20 10 Interior and Environment regular appropriations act (P.L. 111-88, 123 Stat. 2904, 2972).

During a calendar year, Congress typically considers, at least

- 12 regular appropriations bills for the fiscal year that begins on October 1;
- few continuing resolutions for the same fiscal year; and
- one or more supplementals for the previous fiscal year.

SPENDING CEILINGS FOR APPROPRIATIONS MEASURES

The Congressional Budget Act established a process through which Congress annually sets spending ceilings associated with the budget resolution and enforces those ceilings with parliamentary rules, or *points of order*, during congressional consideration of budgetary legislation, including appropriations bills.

Allocations

As mentioned previously, within each chamber, the total budget authority and outlays included in the annual budget resolution are allocated among the House and Senate committees with jurisdiction over spending, including the House and Senate Committees on Appropriations. Through this allocation process, the budget resolution sets total spending ceilings for each House and Senate committee (referred to as the *302(a) allocations*).[50] **Table 3** provides 3 02(a) allocations to the House Committee on Appropriations for FY20 10.

Table 3 includes allocations for discretionary spending and mandatory spending. Congress divides budget authority and the resulting outlays into two categories: discretionary spending and direct (or mandatory) spending (including net interest[51]). Discretionary spending is controlled by the annual appropriations acts, which are under the jurisdiction of the House and Senate Committees on Appropriations. In contrast, direct spending is controlled by legislation under the jurisdiction of the legislative committees.[52] Appropriations measures include all the discretionary spending as well as budget authority to finance the obligations of some direct spending programs.

Discretionary spending provides funds for a wide variety of activities, such as those described in the "Introduction" above, whereas mandatory spending primarily funds entitlement programs[53] as well as other mandatory spending programs. Of the total outlays for FY2009, 35% was discretionary spending, 60% was mandatory spending, and 5% was net interest.

Table 3. House Committee on Appropriations' 302(a) Allocations for FY20 10 (in Billions of Dollars)

Spending Category	Budget Authority	Outlays
Discretionary	1,082.540	1,269.745
Mandatory	725.056	715.684

Source: U.S. Congress, Conference Committee, *Concurrent Resolution on the Budget for Fiscal Year 2010,* conference report to accompany S.Con.Res. 13, 111th Cong., [1st] sess., April 27, 2009, H.Rept. 111-89 (Washington: GPO, 2009), p. 145.

Regarding the distribution of discretionary spending outlays for FY2009, 53% of the outlays was for defense activities, 43% for domestic activities, and 3% for international activities.[54]

The mandatory spending provided in appropriations measures is predominantly for entitlement programs, referred to as *appropriated entitlements.* These entitlements are funded through a two- step process. First, legislation becomes law that sets program parameters (through eligibility requirements and benefit levels, for example); then the appropriations committees *must* provide the budget authority needed to finance the commitment. The appropriations committees have little control over the amount of budget authority provided, since the amount needed is the result of previously enacted commitments in law.[55]

Congress also controls mandatory spending by controlling budget authority. It does not, however, generally control this form of budget authority by setting specific spending levels. It controls mandatory spending, instead by, establishing parameters for government commitments in permanent law, such as Social Security benefit levels and eligibility requirements.

After the House and Senate Committees on Appropriations receive their 3 02(a) allocations, they separately subdivide their allocations among their subcommittees, providing each subcommittee with a ceiling. These subdivisions are referred to as the *302(b) subdivisions.*[56] Table 4 provides the House Committee on Appropriations' initial 302(b) subdivisions of discretionary, mandatory spending for FY20 10.

Making 302(b) allocations is within the jurisdiction of the House and Senate appropriations committees, and they typically make revisions to reflect action on the appropriations bills.

The spending ceilings associated with the annual budget resolution that apply to appropriations measures are generally for a single fiscal year (the upcoming fiscal year), since appropriations measures are annual.[57] If the budget resolution is significantly delayed (or is never completed), there are no total spending ceilings, 302(a) allocations, or 302(b) subdivisions to enforce until the budget resolution is in place. In such instances, the House and Senate have often adopted separate *deeming resolutions* providing, at least, temporary 3 02(a) allocations, thereby, establishing some enforceable spending ceilings.[58]

When Congress did not adopt a FY2007 budget resolution, both the House and Senate adopted separate deeming resolutions in 2006. The House adopted a special rule[59] that, in part, deemed the House-adopted FY2007 budget resolution[60] and accompanying committee report in effect for enforcement purposes. As a result, the FY2007 total spending ceilings and 3 02(a) allocations (and therefore, subsequent 302(b) allocations) were in effect. The Senate included in a FY2006 supplemental appropriations act a deeming provision that, in part, set FY2007 3 02(a) allocations for the Senate Committee on Appropriations.[61]

Table 4. Initial House Appropriations Committee's 302(b) Allocations for FY20 10 (in Billions of Dollars)

Subcommittee	Discretionary	Mandatory	Total
Agriculture			
New Budget Authority	22.900	99.615	122.515
Outlays	25.000	89.174	114.147
Commerce, Justice, and Science			
New Budget Authority	64.314	0.222	64.536
Outlays	70.655	0.257	70.912
Defense			
New Budget Authority	508.040	0.291	508.331
Outlays	547.500	0.291	547.791
Energy and Water Development			
New Budget Authority	33.300		33.300
Outlays	42.500		42.500
Financial Services and General Government			
New Budget Authority	23.550	20.702	44.252
Outlays	25.200	20.699	45.899
Homeland Security			
New Budget Authority	42.384	1.265	43.649
Outlays	46.062	1.262	47.324
Interior and Environment			
New Budget Authority	32.300	0.442	32.742
Outlays	34.300	0.443	34.743

Table 4. (Continued)

Subcommittee	Discretionary	Mandatory	Total
Labor, Health and Human Services, and Education			
New Budget Authority	160.654	551.512	712.166
Outlays	219.692	552.780	772.472
Legislative Branch			
New Budget Authority	4.700	0.130	4.830
Outlays	4.805	0.130	4.935
Military Construction and Veterans Affairs			
New Budget Authority	76.500	50.735	127.235
Outlays	76.900	50.533	127.433
State and Foreign Operations			
New Budget Authority	48.843	0.142	48.985
Outlays	44.180	0.142	44.322
Transportation and Housing and Urban Development			
New Budget Authority	68.821		68.821
Outlays	134.595		134.595
Total[a]			
New Budget Authority	1,086.306	725.056	1,811.362
Outlays	1,272.100	715.684	1,987.784

Source: U.S. Congress, House Committee on Appropriations, *Report on Suballocation of Budget Allocations for Fiscal Year 2010*, 111th Cong., 1st sess., June 12, 2009, H.Rept. 111-148 (Washington: GPO, 2009), p. 2.

a. Primarily due to adjustments provided for in the FY20 10 budget resolution (S.Con.Res. 13, 111th Cong.) to reflect the Congressional Budget Office's estimates of the President's budget, the total new budget authority and outlays in discretionary spending provided in the 302(b) allocations were increased over the initial 302(a) allocations. New budget authority was increased by $4 billion and outlays by $2 billion.

Enforcement

Certain spending ceilings associated with the budget resolution are enforced through points of order raised on the House and Senate floors when the appropriations measures are considered. These points of order are not self-enforcing. A Representative or Senator must raise a point of order that a measure, amendment, or conference report violates a specific rule. Generally, if a Member raises a point of order (such as those described below), and the presiding officer rules that the measure, amendment, or conference report violates the parliamentary rule, the chamber may not consider it on the floor.

House

Two Congressional Budget Act points of order, 302(f) and 311(a),[62] as well as a separate order in the House,[63] are available to enforce certain spending ceilings associated with the annual budget resolution. The Congressional Budget Act points of order apply to committee-reported appropriations bills,[64] certain non-reported appropriations bills,[65] amendments, and conference reports to these measures during their consideration. If such legislation violates these rules, the legislation or amendment cannot be considered. The separate order also provides a procedure to enforce the 302(b) ceilings for appropriations measures as amended.

The 3 02(f) point of order prohibits floor consideration of a measure, amendment, or conference report providing new budget authority for the upcoming fiscal year that would cause the applicable committee 3 02(a) or subcommittee 302(b) allocations of new budget authority for that fiscal year to be exceeded. The application of this point of order on appropriations legislation is generally limited to discretionary spending (and any changes in direct spending initiated in the appropriations measures).[66] If, for example, the committee-reported FY20 10 agriculture appropriations bill had provided $22.900 billion in new discretionary budget authority, which equals the agriculture subcommittee's 3 02(b) allocation in **Table 4**, any amendment proposing additional new discretionary budget authority would violate the 302(f) point of order.

The 311(a) point of order prohibits floor consideration of legislation providing new budget authority for the upcoming fiscal year that would cause the applicable total budget authority and outlay ceilings in the budget resolution for that fiscal year to be exceeded. As the amounts of all the spending measures considered in the House accumulate, they could potentially reach or exceed these ceilings. This point of order would typically affect the last spending bills to be considered, such as supplemental appropriations measures or the last regular appropriations bills. In the House, the so-called *Fazio Exception*, however, exempts legislation if it would not cause the applicable committee 3 02(a) allocations to be exceeded. [67] If, for example, the pending appropriations legislation would not cause the House Appropriations Committee's 3 02(a) allocations to be exceeded, then the legislation would be exempt from the 311(a) point of order.

Appropriations measures considered on the House floor typically include an amount at or just below the subcommittee 302(b) allocations and, in some cases, the committee 302(a) allocations and the total spending ceilings as well. As a result, amendments that would increase new budget authority in an appropriations measure for certain activities must typically decrease funding for other activities in the pending bill. There are two types of House offset amendments considered in Committee of the Whole: clause 2(f) and reachback (or fetchback) amendments. Under House Rule XXI, *clause 2(f) offset amendments* may be offered that consist of two or more amendments considered together (or en bloc) that would change amounts by directly adding text or changing text in the body of the bill. Taken as a whole the amendment can not increase the total new budget authority or outlays in the pending bill. *Reachback offset amendments* are generally offered at the end of the bill and change funding amounts in the pending bill by reference. These amendments must provide offsets in new budget authority, but not necessarily outlays.[68]

The separate order extends enforcement of 3 02(b) allocations to appropriations bills amended in the Committee of the Whole. Regular appropriations bills and major supplemental appropriations measures are typically considered for amendment in the Committee of the Whole. The order generally establishes a point of order in the Committee of the Whole against a motion to rise and report to the House an appropriations bill that, as amended, exceeds the applicable 302(b) allocation in new budget authority.[69] If the Presiding Officer sustains a point of order against such a motion, the bill does not fall or automatically remain in the Committee of the Whole; instead, the Committee of the Whole must decide, by a vote, whether to adopt the motion even though the amended measure exceeds the allocation.[70] The separate order does not apply to a motion to rise and report proposed after the bill has been read for amendment, if offered by the majority leader (or a designee) pursuant to House Rule XXI, clause 2(d).

The House may waive or suspend these points of order by adopting, by majority vote, a special rule waiving the particular point of order prior to floor consideration of the appropriations legislation.

Senate

Three points of order typically enforce spending ceilings associated with the budget resolution. Two are Congressional Budget Act points of order, as provided in sections 302(f) and 311(a). The Senate application of these rules, however, varies from the House versions. The annual budget resolution in recent years typically established another Senate point of order that enforces separate total discretionary spending ceilings established in the budget resolution.[71] In the Senate, these points of order apply to all appropriations measures, both reported by the committee and as amended on the floor, as well as amendments, motions, and conferences reports to these measures.

The Senate 3 02(f) point of order prohibits floor consideration of such legislation providing new budget authority for the upcoming fiscal year that would cause the applicable 302(b) allocations in new budget authority and outlays for that fiscal year to be exceeded. In contrast to the House, it (1) does not enforce the 302(a) allocations and (2) does enforce the outlay allocations. The 311(a) point of order in the Senate is similar to the House version. The Senate, however, does not provide for an exception similar to the *Fazio Exception* in the House. Section 401 of the FY20 10 budget resolution is an example of budget resolution provisions enforcing discretionary spending ceilings. It prohibited the consideration of legislation that would cause the FY2009 or FY20 10 discretionary spending limits in new budgetary authority or outlays established in the budget resolution to be exceeded.

Additionally, the FY2009 budget resolution includes a point of order still in effect that prohibits language in appropriations legislation that would produce a net increase in the cost of mandatory spending programs.[72]

Senators may make motions to waive these points of order at the time the issue is raised. Currently, a vote of three-fifths of all Senators (60 Senators if there are no vacancies) is required to approve a waiver motion for any of these points of order. A vote to appeal the presiding officer's ruling also requires three-fifths vote of all Senators. These super-majority vote requirements for the 302(f) and 311(a) points are currently scheduled to expire on September 30, 2017.

Emergency Spending

Since 1990, both the House and Senate have, generally, developed procedures to exempt from the above spending ceilings funding for emergencies. These procedures have evolved over time.

In the House and Senate, new budget authority and resulting outlays designated in the legislation as necessary to meet emergency needs are exempt from the 302(f) and 311(a) points of order.[73]

A super-majority vote requirement, however, is needed to utilize the emergency designation exemption in the Senate. A Senator may raise a point of order against an emergency designation in legislation, and a motion to waive the point of order or an appeal of the Presiding Officer's ruling requires a three-fifths vote of all Senators (60 Senators if there are no vacancies). If the

Presiding Officer sustains the point of order, the designation is stricken and then the legislation or amendment may be vulnerable to the various enforceable spending ceilings.

Recently, the House and Senate have provided an exemption for new budgetary authority (and resulting outlays) that is designated for overseas deployment and related activities. In practice, overseas deployment and emergency designations considered in the House may be included in the committee-reported bills and conference reports, but not in floor amendments. Under House precedents these designations are considered legislation on an appropriations bill and, therefore, prohibited under House Rule XXI, clause 2(b) and (c). This language is considered to create new law, which would not otherwise exist.[74] The House, sometimes, adopts a special rule waiving this point of order against emergency and contingency operations designations in the reported bills and conference reports, but not such provisions in floor amendments.

By contrast, under Senate precedents such designations are not considered legislation on an appropriations bill. Emergency designations may be included in Senate floor amendments as well as committee amendments, reported bills, amended bills, and conference reports.

RELATIONSHIP BETWEEN AUTHORIZATION AND APPROPRIATION MEASURES

Congress has established an authorization-appropriation process that provides for two separate types of measures—authorization measures and appropriation measures. These bills perform different functions.

Authorization acts establish, continue, or modify agencies or programs. For example, an authorization act may establish or modify programs within the Department of Defense. An authorization act may also explicitly authorize subsequent appropriations for specific agencies and programs, frequently setting spending ceilings for them. These authorization of appropriations provisions may be permanent, annual, or multi-year authorizations. Annual and multi-year provisions require re-authorizations when they expire. Congress is not required to provide appropriations for an authorized discretionary spending program.

Authorization measures are under the jurisdiction of authorization committees such as the House Committees on Agriculture and Homeland

Security, or the Senate Committees on Armed Services and the Judiciary. Appropriations measures provide new budget authority for programs, activities, or agencies previously authorized.

House and Senate rules enforce separation of these functions into different measures by separating committee jurisdiction over authorization and appropriations bills, and with points of order prohibiting certain provisions in appropriations measures.[75] The House and Senate prohibit, in varying degrees, language in appropriations bills providing unauthorized appropriations or legislation on an appropriations bill. An *unauthorized appropriation* is new budget authority in an appropriations measure (including an amendment or conference report) for agencies or programs with no current authorization, or whose budget authority exceeds the ceiling authorized. *Legislation* refers to language in appropriations measures that change existing law, such as establishing new law, or amending or repealing current law. Legislation is under the jurisdiction of the authorizing committees (also called legislative committees).

House rules prohibit unauthorized appropriations and legislation in regular appropriations bills and supplemental appropriations measures which provide funds for more than one purpose or agency (referred to in the House as *general appropriations bills*). However, House rules do not prohibit such provisions in continuing resolutions. The House prohibition applies to bills reported by the House Appropriations Committee, amendments, and conference reports. The House may adopt a special rule waiving this rule prior to floor consideration of the appropriations bill or conference report.[76] The point of order applies to the text of the bill, as well as any amendments or conference reports.

In the Senate, unauthorized appropriations and legislation are treated differently. The Senate rule regarding such language applies to regular bills, supplementals which provide funds for more than one purpose or agency, and continuing resolutions (referred to in the Senate as *general appropriations bills*).

This Senate rule applies only to amendments to general appropriations bills, such as, those

- introduced on the Senate floor;
- reported by the Senate Appropriations Committee to the House-passed measure; or
- proposed as a substitute for the House-passed text.[77]

The rule does not apply to provisions in Senate bills or conference reports. For example, this rule did not apply to provisions in S. 1005, the FY1 998 Defense appropriations bill, as reported by the Senate Appropriations Committee. But it did apply to provisions in H.R. 2107, the FY1998 Interior bill, as reported by the Senate Appropriations Committee, since this version of the bill consisted of amendments to the House-passed bill. [78] Recently, the Senate has adopted unanimous consent agreements, on a bill-by-bill basis, that make these points of order applicable to the provisions of Senate originated appropriations bills.

The Senate rule is less restrictive than the House regarding what is prohibited as unauthorized appropriations. For example, the Senate Appropriations Committee may report committee amendments containing unauthorized appropriations. Similarly, an amendment moved by direction of the committee with legislative jurisdiction or in pursuance of an estimate submitted in accordance with law would not be prohibited as unauthorized. An appropriation also is considered authorized if the Senate has previously passed the authorization during the same session of Congress. In contrast, in the House, the authorization must be in law. As a result, while the Senate rule generally prohibits unauthorized appropriations, Senators rarely raise this point of order because of these exceptions to the rule.

The Senate rule prohibits legislation in both Senate Appropriations Committee amendments and non-committee amendments.[79] It also prohibits non-germane amendments.

The division between an authorization and an appropriation applies only to congressional consideration. If unauthorized appropriations or legislation remain in an appropriations measure as enacted, either because no one raised a point of order or the House or Senate waived the rules, the provision will have the force of law. Unauthorized appropriations, if enacted, are generally available for obligation or expenditure.

RESCISSIONS

Rescissions cancel previously enacted budget authority. For example, if Congress provided $1.6 billion to construct a submarine, it could enact subsequent legislation canceling all or part of the budget authority prior to its obligation. Rescissions are an expression of changed or differing priorities.

They may also be used to offset increases in budget authority for other activities.

The President may recommend rescissions to Congress, but it is up to Congress to act on them. Under Title X of the Congressional Budget Act,[80] if Congress does not enact a bill approving the President's rescissions within 45 days of continuous session of Congress, the budget authority must be made available for obligation.

In response to the President's recommendation, Congress may decide not to approve the amount specified by the President, approve the total amount, or approve a different amount. For example, in 2005, the President requested a rescission of $106 million from the Department of Defense (DOD), Operations and Maintenance, Defense-Wide account and $48.6 million from DOD, Research, Development, Test, and Evaluation, Army account. Congress provided a rescission of $80 million from the first account in the Department of Defense, Emergency Supplemental Appropriations to Address Hurricanes in the Gulf of Mexico, and Pandemic Influenza Act, 2006.[81] The act did not provide a rescission from the second account.

Congress may also initiate rescissions. In the above Act, Congress also included a rescission of $10 million from the Department of State, Diplomatic and Consular Programs account.

As budget authority providing the funding must be enacted into law, so, too, a rescission canceling the budget authority must be enacted into law. Rescissions can be included either in separate rescission measures or any of the three types of appropriations measures.

End Notes

[1] U.S. Constitution, Article I, Section 9.
[2] 31 U.S.C. §§ 1341(a)-1342 and 1349-1350.
[3] 31 U.S.C. § 1301(a).
[4] The House has an additional subcommittee, Select Intelligence Oversight Panel (select panel). It, however, does not have jurisdiction over providing spending. The select panel, instead, makes annual intelligence funding recommendations to the House Defense Appropriations Subcommittee, which has jurisdiction over legislation to provide intelligence spending.
[5] Each appropriations committee provides its subcommittees' jurisdictions on its website; House appropriations subcommittees' jurisdictions are available at http://appropriations.house.gov/ and Senate subcommittees' jurisdictions are available at http://appropriations.senate.gov/.
[6] For additional information, see CRS Report RL3 1572, *Appropriations Subcommittee Structure: History of Changes from 1920-2007*, by James V. Saturno.
[7] Congress generally provides spending for fiscal years, in contrast to calendar years. Federal government *fiscal years* begin on October 1 and end the following September 30. FY20 11 began on October 1, 2010.

[8] 31 U.S.C. § 1105(a).

[9] For information on deadline extensions in presidential transition years, see CRS Report RS20752, *Submission of the President's Budget in Transition Years*, by Robert Keith.

[10] P.L. 111-88, 123 Stat. 2904

[11] 2 U.S.C. § 621 et seq.

[12] Budget resolutions are under the jurisdiction of the House and Senate Committees on the Budget.

[13] The committee ceilings are usually provided in the joint explanatory statement that accompanies the conference report to the budget resolution.

[14] See "Allocations" below.

[15] For more details, see "Spending Ceilings for Appropriations Measures" below.

[16] For more information on budget resolutions, see CRS Report RL3 0297, *Congressional Budget Resolutions: Historical Information*, by Bill Heniff Jr. and Justin Murray.

[17] 2 U.S.C. § 634 (or Congressional Budget Act, section 303); and H.Res. 5, §3(a)(2) (11 1th Cong.).

[18] This exception applies to regular appropriations bills and supplemental appropriations measures that provide funding for more than one agency or purpose (for more information, see "Types of Appropriations Measures" below).

[19] For information on deeming resolutions, see "Allocations" section below and CRS Report RL3 1443, *The "Deeming Resolution": A Budget Enforcement Tool*, by Megan Suzanne Lynch.

[20] For almost 35 years (1971-2004), Congress generally considered 13 regular appropriations bills each year. As a result of two reorganizations of the House and Senate Committees on Appropriations in 2005 and, again, in 2007, the total number of bills changed twice. Congress considered 11 regular bills for FY2006 and FY2007 and 12 bills for FY2008 through FY2010. (For more information, CRS Report RL3 1572, *Appropriations Subcommittee Structure: History of Changes from 1920-2007*, by James V. Saturno.)

[21] Significant anomalies occurred recently. Out of twelve regular bills, the House Appropriations Committee reported five FY2009 regular bills and two FY20 11 regular bills.

[22] Again, anomalies occurred for FY2009 and FY20 11 regular bills. The House passed one FY2009 regular bill and two FY20 11 regular bills.

[23] See "Regular Appropriations Bills" below.

[24] The Senate Appropriations Committee, however, reported nine out of twelve FY2009 regular appropriations bills.

[25] The Senate passed six out of thirteen FY2005 regular bills, three out of eleven FY2007 regular bills, and passed no FY2009 and FY20 11 regular bills. Additionally, it passed seven out of twelve FY2008 regular bills.

[26] For a description of continuing resolutions, see "Continuing Resolutions" below.

[27] At the time of this writing, the FY20 11 regular bills were not completed.

[28] The chair usually proposes a draft bill (the *chair's mark*). The chair and other subcommittee members discuss amendments to the draft and may agree to include some (referred to as *marking up the bill*). Regular appropriations bills are not introduced prior to full committee markup. The bill is introduced when the House appropriations committee reports the bill; a bill number is assigned at that time. House rules allow the House appropriations committee to originate a bill. In contrast, most House committees do not have such authority.

[29] Because the regular appropriations bills must be completed in a timely fashion, House Rule XIII, clause 5, provides that these appropriations bills are privileged. This allows the House Committee on Appropriations to make a motion to bring a regular appropriations bill directly to the floor in contrast to asking the Rules Committee to report a special rule providing for the measure's consideration, as is necessary for most major bills.
In recent years, the House appropriations committee has usually used the special rule procedure, however. These special rules typically include waivers of certain parliamentary rules regarding the consideration of appropriations bills and certain provisions within them. Special rules may also be used for other purposes, such as restricting floor amendments.

[30] House Rule XVIII, clause 3, requires that appropriations measures be considered in the Committee of the Whole before the House votes on passage of the measures (see CRS Report 95-563, *The Legislative Process on the House Floor: An Introduction*, by Christopher M. Davis; and CRS Report RL32200, *Debate, Motions, and Other Actions in the Committee of the Whole*, by Bill Heniff Jr. and Elizabeth Rybicki.

[31] *A ranking minority member* of a committee or subcommittee is the head of the minority party members of the particular committee or subcommittee.

[32] For more information, see CRS Report 98-995, *The Amending Process in the House of Representatives*, by Christopher M. Davis.

[33] Under *unanimous consent agreements*, the House agrees to the new parameters if no Representative objects.

[34] Recently, in cases in which the non-traditional practice is used, the Senate Committee on Appropriations typically reports an original Senate bill, the Senate waits for the House to send its bill to the Senate. After it arrives, the Senate considers the text of the original Senate bill as a complete substitute amendment to the House-passed bill, considers additional amendments, and then generally passes the House-passed bill, as amended.

[35] The Senate may waive these rules either by unanimous consent or, in some cases, by motion.

[36] If the Senate and/or House does not pass a bill, informal negotiations may take place on the basis of the reported version of that chamber(s). For example, the provisions of the House-passed bill and Senate committee-reported bill might be negotiated. Typically, the compromise is included in a conference report on an omnibus appropriations measure (see "Regular Appropriations Bills" section below).

[37] House Rule XXII, clause 9, and Senate Rule XXVIII, paragraphs 2 and 3.

[38] Senate Rule XLIV, paragraph 8.

[39] For more detailed information on these Senate rules, see. CRS Report RS22733, *Senate Rules Restricting the Content of Conference Reports*, by Elizabeth Rybicki.

[40] If either house rejects the conference report, the two houses normally agree to further conference, usually appointing the same conferees.

[41] U.S. Constitution, Article I, section 7.

[42] A notable exception was an FY2007 continuing resolution (P.L. 110-5, 121 Stat. 8), which provided funding for nine FY2007 regular appropriations bills through the end of FY2007.

[43] The term *report language* refers to information provided in reports accompanying committee-reported legislation as well as joint explanatory statements, which are included in conference reports. Although the entire document is generally referred to as a conference report, it comprises two separate parts. The conference report contains a conference committee's proposal for legislative language resolving the House and Senate differences on a measure, while the joint explanatory statement explains the conference report.

[44] Authorization measures may also provide transfer authority. For information on authorization measures, see "Relationship Between Authorization and Appropriation Measures" below.

[45] Transfer authority may be required, however, in cases in which the appropriations act includes a set aside for a specified activity within an account.

[46] For example, five FY2010 regular appropriations bills were attached to the FY2010 Transportation and Housing and Urban Development regular appropriations act (P.L. 111-117, 123 Stat. 3034).

[47] There is no agreed upon definition of omnibus appropriations measure, but the term *minibus appropriations measure* has sometimes been used to refer to a measure including only a few regular appropriations bills, while *omnibus appropriations measure* refers to a measure containing several regular bills.

[48] In a few cases, Congress resolved their differences through an exchange of amendments (for more information on this process, see CRS Report R41003, *Amendments Between the Houses: Procedural Options and Effects*, by Elizabeth Rybicki).

[49] Congress initially considered the FY2009 regular bills during President George W. Bush's last year in office (2008), but completed the process the following calendar year (2009), during the first year of President Barack H. Obama's presidency.

[50] This refers to section 3 02(a) of the Congressional Budget Act. Typically, these are provided in the joint explanatory statement that accompanies the conference report on the budget resolution.

[51] "In the federal budget, net interest comprises the government's interest payments on debt held by the public, offset by interest income that the government receives on loans and cash balances and by earnings of the National Railroad Retirement Investment Trust." U.S. Congressional Budget Office, *Glossary of Budgetary and Economic Terms*, available at http://www.cbo.gov.

[52] For example, Social Security and Medicare Part A are under the jurisdiction of the House Committee on Ways and Means and Senate Committee on Finance. Most standing committees are legislative committees, such as the House Committee on Armed Services and the Senate Committee on the Judiciary. For more information, see "Relationship Between Authorization and Appropriation Measures" below.

[53] The Congressional Budget Office defines entitlement as: A legal obligation of the federal government to make payments to a person, group of people, business, unit of government, or similar entity that meets the eligibility criteria set in law and for which the budget authority is not provided in advance in an appropriation act. Spending for entitlement programs is controlled through those programs' eligibility criteria and benefit or payment rules. The best- known entitlements are the government's major benefit programs, such as Social Security and Medicare. U.S. Congressional Budget Office, *Glossary of Budgetary and Economic Terms*, available at http://www.cbo.gov.

[54] Due to rounding, the total percentage is 99%.

[55] Some mandatory spending is provided through a one-step process in which the authorization act sets the program parameters and provides the budget authority, such as Social Security.

[56] This refers to section 302(b) of the Congressional Budget Act.

[57] In contrast, spending ceilings associated with the budget resolution that apply to legislative measures are generally provided for several fiscal years.

[58] For more information, see CRS Report RL3 1443, *The "Deeming Resolution": A Budget Enforcement Tool*, by Megan Suzanne Lynch.

[59] H.Res. 818, §2 (109th Cong).

[60] H.Con.Res. 376 (109th Cong.).

[61] P.L. 109-234, §7035(a); 120 Stat. 418.

[62] These refer to sections 302(f) and 311(a), respectively, of the Congressional Budget Act (see also, H.Res. 5, §3(a)(4), 111th Cong.).

[63] A *separate order* is a provision that is not a part of the House Standing Rules, but is provided under the rulemaking authority of the House. H.Res. 5, §3(a)(4), 111th Cong.) established the separate order, which is the same as separate orders established in the 109th Congress (H.Res. 248, §2) and, again, in the 1 10th Congress (H.Res. 6, §51 1(a)(5)).

[64] The House Committee on Appropriations almost always reports regular and major supplemental appropriations bills. It, however, does not generally report continuing resolutions.

[65] If a special rule expedites consideration of a measure by ordering the previous question directly to passage, the form of the measure considered is subject to the points of order. Some continuing resolutions are considered by this procedure.

[66] The point of order does not apply to increases in direct spending required under current law.

[67] Section 311(c) of the Congressional Budget Act. The title of the exception refers to former Representative Victor Herbert Fazio, Jr. (CA).

[68] For more information, see CRS Report RL3 1055, *House Offset Amendments to Appropriations Bills: Procedural Considerations*, by Sandy Streeter.

[69] For more detailed information on motions to rise, CRS Report RL32200, *Debate, Motions, and Other Actions in the Committee of the Whole*, by Bill Heniff Jr. and Elizabeth Rybicki.

[70] If the committee votes against "rising," it may consider one proper amendment, such as an amendment reducing funds in the bill to bring it into compliance with the allocation. The separate order also provides an up-or-down vote on the amendment. Only one such point of order may be raised against a single measure.

[71] For example, section 401(a) and (b) of the FY2010 budget resolution (S.Con.Res. 13, 111th Cong.), included such spending limits and a point of order for FY2009 and FY2010.

[72] See S.Con.Res. 70, §314 (110th Cong.).

[73] House exemption provided in section 423(b) of the FY2010 budget resolution (S.Con.Res. 13, 111th Cong.); Senate exemption included in section 403 of the same measure.

[74] Specifically, *special budgetary designations pursuant to the concurrent resolution on the budget* are considered "legislation on an appropriations bill." Special budgetary designations include provisions (1) designating funds for "overseas deployment and other activities" under section 423(a) of S.Con.Res. 13 (11 1th Cong.); and (2) designating funds as "an emergency requirement" under section 423(b) of the same resolution. For more information on legislation on an appropriations bill, see "Relationship Between Authorization and Appropriation Measures" section below.

[75] House Rule XXI, clause 2; House Rule XXII, clause 5; and Senate Rule XVI. House rules also prohibit appropriations in authorization measures, amendments, or conference reports (Rule XXI, clause 4 and House Rule XXII, clause 5).

[76] The special rule may provide a waiver for specified provisions or all provisions in the bill that are subject to the point of order. The special rule may also provide a waiver for specific amendments. Special rules typically waive points of order against all provisions in all conference reports on general appropriations measures.

[77] The Senate rules also applies to amendments between the houses.

[78] The Senate rule reflects Senate practices at the time the rule was established. The Senate Appropriations Committee traditionally reported numerous amendments to the House-passed appropriations bill, instead of reporting an original Senate bill. Therefore, the rule's prohibition only applies to amendments, both committee and floor amendments.

[79] Under Senate precedents, an amendment containing legislation may be considered if it is germane to language in the House-passed appropriations bill. That is, if the House opens the door by including a legislative provision in an appropriations bill, the Senate has an "inherent right" to amend it. However, if the Senate considers an original Senate bill, rather than the House-passed bill with amendments, there is no House language to which the legislative provision could be germane. Therefore, the *defense of germaneness* is not available.

[80] Title X is referred to as the Impoundment Control Act.

[81] P.L. 109-148, 119 Stat. 2680.

In: Overview of Congressional Appropriations   ISBN: 978-1-61209-849-4
Editors: J.M. Stewart, D.M. Allworth   © 2011 Nova Science Publishers, Inc.

Chapter 2

ADVANCE APPROPRIATIONS, FORWARD FUNDING, AND ADVANCE FUNDING

Sandy Streeter

Apppropriations acts generally make budget authority (or BA)[1] available for use (or obligation) at the start of the fiscal year covered by the act. For example, the FY2010 appropriations acts generally made budget authority available on October 1, 2009.[2] Sometimes appropriations bills provide a different date for specified budget authority within the act to become first available so that the funding cycle does not coincide with the fiscal year generally covered by the act. There are three types of this kind of budget authority: advance appropriations, forward funding, and advance funding.

ADVANCE APPROPRIATIONS

Advance appropriations means that budget authority will become available one or more fiscal years after the fiscal year covered by the act. An FY2010 appropriations act, for example, provided specific funds for certain activities that were not available until October 1, 201 0—the start of FY2011. The act also provided funds for specific activities that will not be available until the start of FY20 12.

For purposes of enforcement, appropriations are generally *scored*[3] in the fiscal year the funds first become available. Therefore, an advance appropriation (and resulting outlays) for FY2011 that was provided in an FY2010 appropriations act would be included for calculating total budget authority and outlays for FY2011, but not FY2010. The budget authority and outlays would not be included in calculations to determine if the appropriations act violated FY2010 spending ceilings established under the Congressional Budget and Impoundment Control Act of 1974[4] or additional spending ceilings associated with the annual budget resolution.[5] During times of budgetary constraint, therefore, advance appropriations may be used to provide spending that would be counted against future, rather than current, limits.

In response to concern about this, Congress typically includes in the annual budget resolution a total spending ceiling for most advance appropriations and identifies those accounts that may be funded through advance appropriations. The budget resolutions provide for similar Senate and House enforcement mechanisms during floor consideration of appropriations measures.[6]

FORWARD FUNDING

Forward funding is a term that applies to budget authority that generally becomes available for obligation in the last quarter of the fiscal year of the appropriations act and whose availability continues the following fiscal year. Forward funding in an FY2010 appropriations act may have provided that the budget authority for specified activities would not become available until July 1, 2010, and remain available through FY2011.

This budget authority is scored in the fiscal year in which it first becomes available. Budget authority in an FY2010 appropriations act would be included in the FY2010 calculations. Since forward funding generally becomes available near the end of the fiscal year, the Office of Management and Budget (OMB) and Congressional Budget Office (CBO) may estimate[7] that most of the outlays will occur in subsequent fiscal years. Such forward funding outlays would not be scored for the first fiscal year, but would be scored for subsequent fiscal years in which they are projected to occur.

ADVANCE FUNDING

Advance funding is budget authority authorizing obligations late in the fiscal year, if needed. However, unless used, the budget authority is charged to the succeeding fiscal year. Advance funding is contingency funding for a few programs that require federal payments in which the funds are borrowed from the succeeding fiscal year.

Advance funding is used to fund benefit payments that are difficult to predict, such as unemployment compensation. An appropriations act would provide a specific amount of budget authority, but would also state that, if needed, an agency may obligate additional funds to meet benefit needs. If advance funding is used, budget authority for that fiscal year is increased by the amount obligated and budget authority for the succeeding fiscal year is reduced by that amount.

End Notes

[1] *Budget authority* is the authority provided by federal law to incur financial obligations that will result in immediate or future expenditures (or outlays) involving federal funds. Examples of financial obligations are entering into a contract to build a submarine or purchase supplies.

[2] The principle applies even in cases in which all the regular appropriations bills are not enacted by October 1.

[3] Scoring refers to estimates of budget authority, outlays, revenues, and deficit levels resulting from congressional budgetary action. These estimates are usually prepared by the Congressional Budget Office and Office of Management and Budget and compare congressional action to targets and ceilings, such as budget resolution spending ceilings.

[4] 2 U.S.C. 621-645; P.L. 93-344, as amended. In particular, section 311 establishes a point of order against spending that breaches the total spending level established in the budget resolution, and section 302 establishes a point of order against spending that would breach a committee's spending allocation. Section 303 of the Congressional Budget Act exempts certain advanced appropriations from the prohibition against considering spending legislation until after Congress has agreed to the budget resolution for the fiscal year. For more information on Congressional Budget Act points of order, see CRS Report 97-684, *The Congressional Appropriations Process: An Introduction*, by Sandy Streeter, and CRS Report 97-865, *Points of Order in the Congressional Budget Process*, by James V. Saturno.

[5] For example, see section 401 of S.Con.Res. 13 (111th Cong.) established a point of order in the Senate against discretionary spending in excess of specified levels for FY2009 and FY2010.

[6] For an example, see sections 402 and 424 of S.Con.Res. 13 (111th Cong.), Concurrent Resolution on the Budget for Fiscal Year 2010.

[7] Outlay estimates are used in scoring appropriations measures and in calculating the federal deficit. Information on actual outlays is not available until the fiscal year is completed. OMB and CBO provide outlay estimates for each appropriation based on historical patterns.

In: Overview of Congressional Appropriations   ISBN: 978-1-61209-849-4
Editors: J.M. Stewart, D.M. Allworth   © 2011 Nova Science Publishers, Inc.

Chapter 3

OMNIBUS APPROPRIATIONS ACTS: OVERVIEW OF RECENT PRACTICES

Jessica Tollestrup

SUMMARY

Omnibus appropriations acts have become a significant feature of the legislative process in recent years as Congress and the President have used them more frequently to bring action on the regular appropriations cycle to a close. Following a discussion of pertinent background information, this report reviews the recent enactment of such measures and briefly addresses several issues raised by their use.

For nearly two centuries, regular appropriations acts were considered by the House and Senate as individual measures and enacted into law as freestanding laws. In 1950, the House and Senate undertook a one-time experiment in improving legislative efficiency by considering all of the regular appropriations acts for FY1951 in a single bill, the Omnibus Appropriations Act of 1950. The following year, the House and Senate returned to the practice of considering the regular appropriations acts individually.

During the 25-year period covering FY1986-FY2010, a total of 318 regular appropriations acts were considered that were eventually enacted into law. Of these, 190 (58.5%) were enacted as freestanding measures and 128 (41.5%) were enacted in omnibus legislation. On average, each year nearly eight (7.6) regular appropriations acts were enacted into law as freestanding measures and about five (5.1) were enacted into law in omnibus legislation.

During this period, 17 different omnibus measures were enacted into law for 15 different fiscal years (two separate omnibus appropriations acts were enacted for both FY2001 and FY2009). Each of the measures funded between two and 13 regular appropriations acts, on average funding over seven (7.5) of them.

Twelve of the omnibus measures were bills or joint resolutions carrying the designation "omnibus," "consolidated," or "omnibus consolidated" appropriations in the title; four were continuing appropriations acts (FY1986, FY1987, FY1988, and FY2009); one was a continuing resolution (FY2007); and one was the VA-HUD Appropriations Act for FY2001, which also included the Energy and Water Development Appropriations Act for FY2001.

In addition to the customary concern—of sacrificing the opportunity for debate and amendment for greater legislative efficiency—that arises whenever complex legislation is considered under time constraints, the use of omnibus appropriations acts has generated controversy for other reasons. These include whether adequate consideration was given to regular appropriations acts prior to their incorporation into omnibus appropriations legislation, the use of across-the-board spending cuts, and the inclusion of significant legislative (rather than funding) provisions.

This report will be updated as warranted.

Omnibus appropriations acts have become a significant feature of the legislative process in Orecent years as Congress and the President have resorted more frequently to their use to bring action on the regular appropriations cycle to a close. Following a discussion of pertinent background information, this report reviews the recent use of such measures and briefly addresses several issues that their use raises.

BACKGROUND

Each year, Congress and the President enact discretionary spending[1] in the form of regular appropriations acts, as well as continuing and supplemental appropriations acts.[2] The number of regular appropriations acts had been fixed at 13 for several decades,[3] but a realignment of the House and Senate Appropriations subcommittees at the beginning of the 109th Congress reduced the number of regular appropriations acts normally considered each year to 11 (starting with the FY2006 cycle).[4] The number of regular appropriations acts was increased to 12 at the beginning of the 110th Congress (starting with the FY2008 cycle) due to further subcommittee realignment and has remained at that level for the 111th Congress.

If action is not completed on all of the regular appropriations acts toward the end of a congressional session, Congress sometimes will combine the unfinished appropriations acts into an omnibus measure. In some instances, action on the unfinished appropriations acts carries over into the following session. An omnibus act may set forth the full text of each of the regular appropriations acts included therein, or it may enact them individually by cross-reference. For omnibus bills that take the form of continuing resolutions, however, it is important to distinguish between those that provide spending authority for more than one designated area based on a rate, versus those that combine full appropriations bills (either in text or via cross-reference) into a single package. Only those in the later class are counted as omnibus appropriations acts.

The House and Senate consider annual appropriations acts, and other budgetary legislation, within constraints established in a yearly budget resolution required by the Congressional Budget Act of 1974, as amended. Budget resolution policies are enforced by points of order that may be raised during House and Senate consideration of spending, revenue, and debt-limit legislation.[5] On occasion, budget policies may be modified by agreements reached between congressional leaders and the President; such modifications may be accommodated during legislative action through the use of waivers of points of order, emergency spending designations, and other budgetary or procedural devices.

During the period covering FY1991-FY2002, legislative action on annual appropriations acts also was subject to limits on discretionary spending established by the Budget Enforcement Act (BEA) of 1990, as amended. Under this statutory mechanism, separate discretionary spending limits were applied to two different measurements of spending—budget authority and outlays. The discretionary spending limits were enforced by the sequestration process, which involved automatic, largely across-the-board reductions in discretionary spending in order to eliminate any breach of the limits.[6]

For nearly two centuries, regular appropriations acts were considered by the House and Senate as individual measures and enacted into law by the President as freestanding laws. In 1950, the House and Senate undertook a one-time experiment in improving legislative efficiency by considering all of the regular appropriations acts for FY1951 in a single bill, the Omnibus Appropriations Act of 1950 (81st Congress, P.L. 759, September 6, 1950).[7] The following year, the House and Senate returned to the practice of considering the regular appropriations acts individually.

Beginning in the late 1970s, continuing appropriations acts sometimes have taken the form of omnibus legislation, generally incorporating the full text of multiple regular appropriations acts for full-year funding instead of providing short-term funding by formula.[8] In recent years, the House and Senate on several occasions have combined multiple regular appropriations acts into "consolidated" appropriations measures, sometimes enacting individual bills by cross-reference.

OMNIBUS APPROPRIATIONS ACTS: FY1986-FY2010

During the 25-year period covering FY1986-FY2010, 17 different omnibus measures were enacted into law for 15 different fiscal years (two separate omnibus appropriations acts were enacted for both FY2001 and FY2009). The 17 omnibus appropriations acts covered a total of 128 regular appropriations acts. Each of the measures funded between two and 13 regular appropriations acts, on average funding over seven (7.5) of them.

Twelve of the omnibus measures were bills or joint resolutions carrying the designation "omnibus," "consolidated," or "omnibus consolidated" appropriations in the title; four were continuing appropriations acts (FY1986, FY1987, FY1988, and FY2009); one was a continuing resolution (FY2007); and one was the VA-HUD Appropriations Act for FY2001, which also included the Energy and Water Development Appropriations Act for FY2001 (see **Table 1**, and, at the end of the report, **Table 3**).

P.L. 110-5, the Revised Continuing Appropriations Resolution for FY2007, did not include the text of the regular appropriations acts that it covered; however, in addition to its formulaic funding provisions, it included many adjustments in appropriated levels and other provisions (amounting to more than 50 pages in length as a slip law), so it is counted as an omnibus appropriations act for purposes of this report.

P.L. 106-553 was enacted as an omnibus measure, enacting the Commerce-Justice-State-Judiciary Appropriations Act for FY2001 and the District of Columbia Appropriations Act for FY2001 by cross-reference. However, the provision dealing with District of Columbia appropriations was repealed; therefore, P.L. 106-553 is not counted in this report as an omnibus measure.

Table 1. Omnibus Appropriations Acts: FY1986-FY2010

1. Further Continuing Appropriations Act, 1986 (P.L. 99-190; December 19, 1985)
2. Continuing Appropriations Act, 1987 (P.L. 99-500; October 18, 1986)
3. Further Continuing Appropriations Act, 1988 (P.L. 100-202; December 22, 1987)
4. Omnibus Consolidated Rescissions and Appropriations Act of 1996 (P.L. 104-134; April 26, 1996)
5. Omnibus Consolidated Appropriations Act, 1997 (P.L. 104-208; September 30, 1996)
6. Omnibus Consolidated and Emergency Supplemental Appropriations Act, 1999 (P.L. 105-277; October 21, 1998)
7. Consolidated Appropriations Act, 2000 (P.L. 106-113; November 29, 1999)
8. Consolidated Appropriations Act, 2001 (P.L. 106-554; December 21, 2000)
9. VA-HUD Appropriations Act, 2001 (P.L. 106-377; October 27, 2000)
10. Consolidated Appropriations Resolution, 2003 (P.L. 108-7; February 20, 2003)
11. Consolidated Appropriations Act, 2004 (P.L. 108-199; January 23, 2004)
12. Consolidated Appropriations Act, 2005 (P.L. 108-447; December 8, 2004)
13. Revised Continuing Appropriations Resolution, 2007 (P.L. 110-5; February 15, 2007)
14. Consolidated Appropriations Act, 2008 (P.L. 110-161; December 26, 2007)
15. Consolidated Security, Disaster Assistance, and Continuing Appropriations Act, 2009 (P.L. 110-329; September 30, 2008)
16. Omnibus Appropriations Act, 2009 (P.L. 111-8; March 11, 2009)
17. Consolidated Appropriations Act, 2010 (P.L. 111-17; December 16, 2009)

Source: Prepared by the Congressional Research Service.

During this period, a total of 319 regular appropriations acts were considered. All but one of these acts were enacted into law either individually or as part of an omnibus measure.[9]

Of the 318 measures enacted into law, 190 (58.5%) were enacted as freestanding measures and 128 (41.5%) were enacted in omnibus legislation. On average, each year nearly eight (7.6) regular appropriations acts were enacted into law as freestanding measures and about five (5.1) were enacted into law in omnibus legislation.

Fifty-six (17.6%) of the 318 regular appropriations acts were enacted into law before October 1, the start of the fiscal year. Nine of these measures were included in an omnibus measure (six in FY1997 and three in FY2009) and the rest were enacted as freestanding measures. On average, less than three (2.2) regular appropriations acts each year were enacted before the start of the fiscal year during this period.

Eight of the 12 omnibus appropriations acts bearing the designation "omnibus," "consolidated," or "omnibus consolidated" in their title originated in the House as a regular appropriations act and were expanded in coverage (and their titles redesignated) at the stage of resolving House-Senate differences. These included the appropriations acts for

- Defense (H.R. 3610) in FY1997;
- Transportation (H.R. 4238) in FY1999;
- District of Columbia (H.R. 3194) in FY2000;
- Labor-HHS-Education (H.R. 4577) in FY2001;
- Agriculture (H.R. 2673) in FY2004;
- Foreign Operations (H.R. 4818) in FY2005;
- State-Foreign Operations (H.R. 2764) in FY2008; and
- Transportation, Housing and Urban Development (H.R. 3288) in FY2010.

In the case of the FY1997, FY1999, FY2000, FY2001, FY2004, FY2005 and FY2010 omnibus appropriations acts, the transformation from a regular appropriations act into a consolidated appropriations act occurred as part of the conference proceedings between the House and Senate. In the case of the final act listed, for FY2008, conference procedures were not used and the transformation occurred in connection with an exchange of amendments between the two chambers.[10]

The acts for FY2000 and FY2001 enacted regular appropriations measures by cross-reference instead of including their full text (except for FY2000 appropriations for the District of Columbia).[11]

None of the other four omnibus appropriations acts bearing the designation involved the transformation of a regular appropriations act. Three of the acts (one for FY1996 and two for FY2009) originated as an omnibus measure and retained this status throughout its consideration. In FY2003, the omnibus measure originated in the House as a simple continuing resolution (H.J.Res. 2), but was expanded in coverage and redesignated during Senate floor action.

SELECTED ISSUES IN THE USE OF OMNIBUS APPROPRIATIONS ACTS

Several issues pertaining to the use of omnibus appropriations have been the focus of debate in recent years, including the extent to which the regular appropriations acts have received consideration prior to being incorporated into omnibus legislation, the use of across-the-board spending cuts, and the inclusion of legislative provisions.

Prior Consideration of Regular Appropriations Acts

One of the chief concerns regarding the use of omnibus appropriations acts is that it reduces the opportunities Members have to debate and amend the regular appropriations acts that are incorporated therein. This concern may be lessened if the regular appropriations acts eventually incorporated into omnibus legislation are first considered individually on the House and Senate floor.

During the FY1986-FY2010 period, the House was more likely than the Senate to have given prior floor consideration to regular appropriations acts eventually incorporated into omnibus legislation, with the House considering 93 out of the 128 regular appropriations acts while the Senate considered 66 (see Table 2). For both the House and the Senate, between FY1986-FY1999, the majority of appropriations acts that were ultimately incorporated into omnibus legislation received floor consideration each year. However, starting in FY2000, both chambers display a greater tendency to incorporate acts into omnibus legislation that did not receive prior floor consideration. Between FY2000-FY2010, the House failed to consider the majority of legislation that was eventually included in the omnibus package in three of the fiscal years. During this same period, the Senate failed to consider the majority of legislation eventually included in the omnibus six of the years.

FY2009 was particularly notable in this regard. For the first omnibus (composed of the Defense, Homeland Security, and Military Construction/Veteran's Affairs appropriations acts), while the Senate failed to separately consider the Military Construction/Veteran's Affairs act (H.R. 6599), the House considered on the floor all three acts contained within the legislation. For the second omnibus, both the House and the Senate failed to separately consider all nine pieces of appropriations legislation that were eventually included in the final package.

Across-the-Board Spending Cuts

To adhere to restraints imposed by congressional budget resolutions, the discretionary spending limits, and ad hoc budget agreements between congressional leaders and the President, or to meet other purposes, Congress and the President from time to time incorporate across-the-board cuts in discretionary budget authority into annual appropriations acts.[12] During the six fiscal years covering FY2000-FY2010, five government-wide, across-the-board spending cuts were included in omnibus appropriations acts. In addition, an across-the-board cut was included in the Defense Appropriations Act for FY2006, a year in which all of the regular appropriations acts were enacted separately.[13]

The government-wide across-the-board spending cuts included in omnibus appropriations acts ranged in size from 0.22% to 0.80% of covered appropriations, and an estimated $1.1 billion to $3.5 billion in savings:

- the 0.38% cut for FY2000 in P.L. 106-113 saved an estimated $2.4 billion in budget authority;
- the 0.22% cut for FY2001 in P.L. 106-554 saved an estimated $1.1 billion in budget authority;
- the 0.65% cut for FY2003 in P.L. 108-7 saved an estimated $2.6 billion in budget authority;
- the 0.59% cut for FY2004 in P.L. 108-199 saved an estimated $2.8 billion in budget authority; and

Table 2. Prior Floor Consideration of Individual Appropriations Acts

Fiscal Year	House		Senate	
	Considered	Not Considered	Considered	Not Considered
1986	5	2	5	2
1987	13	0	8	5
1988	10	3	10	3
1996	5	0	5	0
1997	6	0	4	2
1999	7	1	6	2
2000	1	4	4	1
2001	0	6	2	4
2003	4	7	2	9
2004	7	0	6	1
2005	8	1	2	7
2007	8	1	2	7
2008	11	0	6	5
2009	3	9	2	10
2010	6	0	3	3
Total:	93	34	66	61

Source: Prepared by the Congressional Research Service.

- the 0.80% cut for FY2005 in P.L. 108-447 saved an estimated $3.5 billion in budget authority.

The 0.59% across-the-board cut in nondefense programs for FY2004 in P.L. 108-199 was accompanied by a requirement that defense appropriations, which were exempt from the 0.59% cut, be reduced by a fixed amount ($1.8 billion). This requirement was repealed by Section 9003(c) of the Defense Appropriations Act for FY2005, which President Bush signed into law on August 5, 2004, as P.L. 108-287 (118 Stat. 951 et. seq.).

Omnibus appropriations acts sometimes include other across-the-board spending cuts that apply to individual appropriations acts, as set forth in separate divisions of the omnibus legislation. P.L. 108-199, for example, included two other requirements for much smaller uniform spending cuts in nondefense programs: (1) a 0.465% cut in funding in the Commerce-Justice-State Appropriations division, estimated to yield $188.7 million in savings;

and (2) a cut of $50 million in administrative expenses for the Departments of Labor, Health and Human Services, and Education.

Further, P.L. 108-447 included three other provisions requiring across-the-board spending cuts focused on particular divisions of the act: (1) a 0.54% cut in the Commerce-Justice-State Appropriations division, estimated to save $229 million; (2) a 0.594% cut in the Interior Appropriations division, estimated to save $120 million; and (3) a cut of $18 million in the Labor-HHS-Education Appropriations division, applicable to administrative and related expenses for departmental management (except for the Food and Drug Administration and the Indian Health Service).

The Consolidated Appropriations Act for FY2008 also employed across-the-board spending cuts, but they were not government wide. Instead, they applied to six of the divisions of the act, ranging in size from 0.25% (legislative branch) to 1.747% (Labor-HHS-Education). The Office of Management and Budget estimated total savings from the cuts (excluding cuts affecting the legislative branch) at $3.357 billion in discretionary budget authority.

The significance of the spending cuts differed with regard to budget enforcement. The FY2000 cut was an integral component of the plan that successfully avoided a sequester at the end of the session. The FY2001 cut contributed to overall discretionary spending being below the statutory limits, but the across-the-board cut proved to be unnecessary in avoiding a sequester. With regard to the FY2003 cut, the House and Senate did not reach agreement on a budget resolution and the statutory discretionary limits had expired the fiscal year before; nonetheless, the across-the-board cut was necessary in adhering to an informal limit reached between congressional leaders and President Bush and avoiding a veto of the omnibus appropriations act. Similarly, the FY2004, FY2005, and FY2008 cuts were necessary to keep the costs of the measures under overall limits acceptable to the President.

Although the across-the-board spending cuts were viewed as essential elements in meeting budget enforcement goals, some Members criticized them as involving a formulaic approach that undermined the process of making deliberate, informed choices regarding appropriate funding levels.

Inclusion of Legislative Provisions

Although House and Senate rules and practices over the decades have promoted the separate consideration of legislation and appropriations, the separation has not been ironclad. In many instances, during the routine operation of the annual appropriations process, minor provisions are included in appropriations acts that technically may be regarded under the rules as legislative in nature, but do not significantly undermine the dichotomy between legislation and appropriations. At other times, however, the legislative provisions included in annual appropriations acts—especially omnibus appropriations acts—have been much more substantial and have represented a deliberate suspension of the usual procedural boundaries.

Both House and Senate rules contain prohibitions against the inclusion of legislation in appropriations bills. Clauses 2(b) and 2(c) of House Rule XXI prohibit the inclusion of legislative provisions on regular appropriations bills reported by the committee or added during the floor process. However, continuing resolutions are not considered by House rules to be regular appropriations bills and thus do not fall under the purview of these restrictions. In the Senate, Rule XVI prohibits the inclusion of legislative provisions in general appropriations legislation, but allows exceptions in specified circumstances. As the rules in the House and Senate barring the inclusion of legislation in appropriations are not self-enforcing, can be waived, and allow some exceptions, omnibus appropriations acts have sometimes been used as vehicles to address substantive legislative concerns.

In recent years, there are many examples of the incorporation of significant legislative provisions within omnibus appropriations acts. The Consolidated Appropriations Resolution for FY2003 (P.L. 108-7) included the Agricultural Assistance Act of 2003, amendments to the Price-Anderson Act and the Homeland Security Act, and provisions dealing with the U.S.-China Economic and Security Review Commission, among other legislative matters. The Consolidated Appropriations Act for FY2008 (P.L. 110-161) included such items as the Emergency Steel Loan Guarantee Act of 1999 Amendments, the Harmful Algal Bloom and Hypoxia Research and Control Act of 1998 Amendments, the ED 1.0 Act, and the Kids in Disasters Well-being, Safety, and Health Act of 2007. Although the inclusion of significant legislative matters may represent an efficient way to conclude legislative business as a congressional session comes to an end, it can also raise concerns as to whether this context provides Members with an adequate opportunity to debate and amend them.

Table 3. Detail on Omnibus Appropriations Acts: FY1986-FY2010

Fiscal Year	Congress/Session[a]	Number of Regular Appropriations Acts:			Omnibus Appropriations Act
		Enacted by Start of Fiscal Year	Enacted as Freestanding Legislation	Enacted in Omnibus Legislation	
1986	99/1	0	6	7	Further Continuing Appropriations Act, FY1986 (P.L. 99-190, December 19, 1985)
1987	99/2	0	0	13	Continuing Appropriations Act, FY1987 (P.L. 99-591, October 18, 1986)
1988	100/1	0	0	13	Further Continuing Appropriations Act, FY1988 (P.L. 100-202, December 22, 1987)
1989	100/2	7	13	0	[none]
1990	101/1	1	13	0	[none]
1991	101/2	0	13	0	[none]
1992	102/1	3	12	0	[none]
1993	102/2	1	13	0	[none]
1994	103/1	2	13	0	[none]
1995	103/2	13	13	0	[none]
1996	104/1	0	8	5	Omnibus Consolidated Rescissions and Appropriations Act of 1996 (P.L. 104-134, April 26, 1996)

Table 3. (Continued)

Fiscal Year	Congress/Session[a]	Number of Regular Appropriations Acts:			Omnibus Appropriations Act
		Enacted by Start of Fiscal Year	Enacted as Freestanding Legislation	Enacted in Omnibus Legislation	
1997	104/2	13	7	6	Omnibus Consolidated Appropriations Act, 1997 (P.L. 104-208, September 30, 1996)
1998	105/1	0	13	0	[none]
1999	105/2	1	5	8	Omnibus Consolidated and Emergency Supplemental Appropriations Act, 1999 (P.L. 105-277; October 21, 1998)
2000	106/1	4	8	5	Consolidated Appropriations Act, 2000 (P.L. 106-113, November 29, 1999)
2001	106/2	2	7	6	Consolidated Appropriations Act, 2001 [3 acts] (P.L. 106-554, December 21, 2000) and VA-HUD Appropriations Act, 2001 [2 acts] (P.L. 106-377, October 27, 2000)
2002	107/1	0	13	0	[none]
2003	107/2	0	2	11	Consolidated Appropriations Resolution, 2003 (P.L. 108-7, February 20, 2003)

Table 3. (Continued)

Fiscal Year	Congress/ Session[a]	Number of Regular Appropriations Acts:			Omnibus Appropriations Act
		Enacted by Start of Fiscal Year	Enacted as Freestanding Legislation	Enacted in Omnibus Legislation	
2004	108/1	2	6	7	Consolidated Appropriations Act, 2004 (P.L. 108-199; January 23, 2004)
2005	108/2	1	4	9	Consolidated Appropriations Act, 2005 (P.L. 108-447; December 8, 2004)
2006	109/1	2	12	0	[none]
2007	109/2	1	2	9	Revised Continuing Appropriations Resolution, 2007 (P.L. 110-5; February 15, 2007)
2008	110/1	0	1	11	Consolidated Appropriations Act, 2008 (P.L. 110-161; December 26, 2007)
2009	110/2	3	0	12	Consolidated Security, Disaster Assistance, and Continuing Appropriations Act, 2009 (P.L. 110-329; September 30, 2008) and Omnibus Appropriations Act, 2009 (P.L. 111-8; March 11, 2009)
2010	111/1	0	6	6	Consolidated Appropriations Act, 2010 (P.L. 111-17; December 16, 2009)

Table 3. (Continued)

Fiscal Year	Congress/Session[a]	Number of Regular Appropriations Acts:			Omnibus Appropriations Act
		Enacted by Start of Fiscal Year	Enacted as Freestanding Legislation	Enacted in Omnibus Legislation	
	Total	56	190	128	—
	Annual Average	2.2	7.6	5.1	—

Source: Calendars of the United States House of Representatives, 99th-111th Congresses, Legislative Information System.

a. In five instances, covering FY1996, FY2003, FY2004, FY2007, and FY2009, omnibus appropriations legislation was not enacted into law until the following session.

Acknowledgments

The original version of this report was written by Robert Keith, formerly a Specialist in American National Government at CRS. The listed author has revised and updated this report and is available to respond to inquiries on the subject.

End Notes

[1] *Discretionary spending*, which accounts for roughly one-third of total federal spending, is spending that is under the control of the House and Senate Appropriations Committees. For the most part, discretionary spending funds the routine operations of the federal government. It is distinguished from *direct spending*, which is controlled by the legislative committees in substantive law and funds such mandatory programs as Social Security and Medicare. Discretionary spending and direct spending together make up total federal spending.

[2] For background on the appropriations process, see CRS Report 97-684, *The Congressional Appropriations Process: An Introduction*, by Sandy Streeter.

[3] For information on changes in the number of regular appropriations acts over the years, see CRS Report RL31572, *Appropriations Subcommittee Structure: History of Changes from 1920-2007*, by James V. Saturno.

[4] The Senate Appropriations Committee reported a twelfth regular appropriations act, for the District of Columbia, but in final legislative action it was incorporated into another bill.

[5] For a general discussion of budget enforcement procedures, see CRS Report 98-721, *Introduction to the Federal Budget Process*, by Robert Keith.

[6] The sequestration process is discussed in detail in CRS Report RL31137, *Sequestration Procedures Under the 1985 Balanced Budget Act*, by Robert Keith.

[7] See "The Omnibus Appropriations Act of 1950," by Dalmus H. Nelson, *Journal of Politics*, vol. 15, no. 2, May 1953.

[8] For more information on practices relating to the use of continuing appropriations acts, see CRS Report RL32614, *Duration of Continuing Resolutions in Recent Years*, by Jessica Tollestrup.

[9] The Foreign Operations Appropriations Act for FY1992 was not enacted into law. Funding for activities covered by this act was provided in a series of continuing resolutions, culminating with the enactment of P.L. 102-266 on April 1, 1992.

[10] For a discussion of legislative action on the FY2008 measure, see CRS Report RL34298, *Consolidated Appropriations Act for FY2008: Brief Overview*, by Robert Keith.

[11] For additional information on the legislative history and structure of recent omnibus appropriations acts, see (1) CRS Report RS20403, *FY2000 Consolidated Appropriations Act: Reference Guide*, by Robert Keith; (2) CRS Report RS20756, *FY2001 Consolidated Appropriations Act: Reference Guide*, by Robert Keith; (3) CRS Report RS21433, *FY2003 Consolidated Appropriations Resolution: Reference Guide*, by Robert Keith; (4) CRS Report RS21684, *FY2004 Consolidated Appropriations Act: Reference Guide*, by Robert Keith; (5) CRS Report RS21983, *FY2005 Consolidated Appropriations Act: Reference Guide*, by Robert Keith; (6) CRS Report RL34298, *Consolidated Appropriations Act for FY2008: Brief Overview*, by Robert Keith; and (7) CRS Report RL34711, *Consolidated Appropriations Act for FY2009 (P.L. 110-329): An Overview*, by Robert Keith.

[12] This topic is discussed in more detail in CRS Report RL32153, *Across-the-Board Spending Cuts in End-of-Session Appropriations Acts*, by Robert Keith.

[13] The act, which became P.L. 109-148 on December 30, 2005, included in Division B, Section 3801(a), a government-wide spending cut of 1% (118 Stat. 2791-2792). Emergency requirements and spending for the Veterans Administration were exempted from the cut, which was expected to reduce total budget authority by about $8.5 billion. For additional information, see OMB Bulletin 06-02, *Guidance on Implementing the Government-wide Across-the-Board Reduction in the Department of Defense Appropriations Act, FY2006 (H.R. 2863)*, January 5, 2006, available at http://www.whitehouse.gov/sites/default/files/omb/assets/omb/bulletins/fy2006/b06-02.pdf

In: Overview of Congressional Appropriations   ISBN: 978-1-61209-849-4
Editors: J.M. Stewart, D.M. Allworth   © 2011 Nova Science Publishers, Inc.

Chapter 4

ANNUAL APPROPRIATIONS ACTS: CONSIDERATION DURING LAME-DUCK SESSIONS

Jessica Tollestrup

SUMMARY

Seven of the past eight Congresses, covering the 103rd Congress through the 110th Congress, have concluded with a lame-duck session (no such session occurred in 1996, during the 104th Congress). The consideration of annual appropriations acts has been an important element of some, but not all, of these lame-duck sessions. Although no annual appropriation acts were considered during lame-duck sessions held in 1994, 1998, and 2008, a total of 14 regular and 11 continuing appropriations acts were considered and subsequently enacted into law during the four other lame-duck sessions held in 2000, 2002, 2004, and 2006.

Although some (and occasionally all) regular appropriations acts may be enacted into law before the start of the fiscal year, in recent decades it has been common for many regular appropriations acts to be enacted after the start of the fiscal year. In the past, this has triggered the necessity for continuing resolutions to extend spending authority until the annual appropriations acts have been enacted. Additionally, this has periodically necessitated the consideration of regular appropriations legislation during the last quarter of the calendar year, or even during the following session.

This report provides information on the consideration of annual appropriations acts in the years that lame-duck sessions occurred between 1994 and 2008 (FY1995, FY1999, FY2001, FY2003, FY2005, FY2007, and FY2009). A lame-duck session occurs during the period following election day, which is the Tuesday after the first Monday in November of each even-numbered year, and before the convening of a new Congress about two months later in early January. Several factors may contribute to the occurrence of lame-duck sessions, including the need to deal with unfinished appropriations or other budgetary matters.

A total of 131 annual appropriations acts—88 regular appropriations acts and 43 continuing appropriations acts—were enacted into law for FY1995-FY2009 before, during, and after the seven most recent lame-duck sessions. With respect to the 88 regular appropriations acts, 45 were enacted into law before the beginning of the applicable lame-duck session, 14 were enacted during the lame-duck session, and 29 were enacted afterwards. With respect to the 43 continuing appropriations acts, 28 were enacted into law before the beginning of the applicable lame-duck session, 11 were enacted during the lame-duck session, and four were enacted afterwards.

The report will be updated as developments warrant.

Although some (and occasionally all) regular appropriations acts may be enacted into law Abefore the start of the fiscal year, in recent decades it has been common for many regular appropriations acts to be enacted after the start of the fiscal year, during the last quarter of the calendar year.[1] In some recent instances, including FY2006 and FY2008, the consideration of regular appropriations acts has carried over to the following session.

Seven of the past eight Congresses, covering the 103rd Congress through the 110th Congress, have concluded with a lame-duck session (no such session occurred in 1996, during the 104th Congress). The consideration of annual appropriations acts has been an important element of some, but not all, of these lame-duck sessions. Although no annual appropriation acts were considered during lame-duck sessions held in 1994, 1998, and 2008, a total of 14 regular and 11 continuing appropriations acts were considered and subsequently enacted into law during the four other lame-duck sessions held in 2000, 2002, 2004, and 2006.

This report provides information on the consideration of annual appropriations acts in connection with lame-duck sessions occurring between 1994 and 2008.

BACKGROUND

A lame-duck session occurs during the period following election day, which is the Tuesday after the first Monday in November of each even-numbered year, and before the convening of a new Congress about two months later in early January. (Under the 20th Amendment to the Constitution, Congress is required to convene at noon on January 3, unless by statute it designates a different day for convening; in recent years, a new Congress has convened during the first week of January in each odd-numbered year, but not necessarily on January 3).[2]

A "lame duck" session of Congress is one that takes place after the election for the next Congress has been held, but before the current Congress has reached the end of its constitutional term. Under contemporary conditions, any meeting of Congress that occurs between a congressional election in November and the following January 3 is a lame duck session. The significant characteristic of a lame duck session is that its participants are the sitting Members of the existing Congress, not those who will be entitled to sit in the new Congress.[3]

Table 1. Party Control of Government During Lame-Duck Sessions: 1994-2008

| Congress | Lame-Duck Session | | Party Control | | |
	Dates	Duration (in days)	Presidency	House	Senate
103rd	11/29-12/1 1994	3	D (Clinton)	D	D
104th	[none]	—	D (Clinton)	R	R
105th	12/17-12/19 1998	3	D (Clinton)	R	R
106th	11/13-12/15 2000	33	D (Clinton)	R	R
107th	11/7-11/22 2002	16	R (GW Bush)	R	D
108th	11/16-12/8 2004	23	R (GW Bush)	R	R
109th	11/9-12/9 2006	31	R (GW Bush)	R	R
110th	11/19-01/03 2009	46	R (GW Bush)	D	D

Source: Prepared by the Congressional Research Service.

Notes: "D" refers to the Democratic Party and "R" refers to the Republican Party. "Duration" refers to the span of days from the first date to the last date that the House, the Senate, or both were in session, not to the number of days that one or both chambers were in session during that period. In 2002, the House and Senate held pro forma sessions without adjourning until the election on November 5; thus, the lame-duck session may be regarded as commencing on the next day of session after the election, November 7, but legislative action did not resume until November 12. In 2006, the House and Senate adjourned early in the morning of December 9 (before 5:00 a.m.).

Several factors may contribute to the occurrence of lame-duck sessions, including the need to deal with unfinished business or urgent matters that have arisen suddenly. The consideration of legislative proposals, particularly those with significant budgetary implications, sometimes is postponed until a lame-duck session, often to avoid the need for politically difficult votes before an election. Consideration of a measure raising the statutory limit on the public debt by $800 billion (to $8.184 trillion), for example, was postponed in 2004 until the lame-duck session; the measure was signed into law by President George W. Bush on November 19, 2004 as P.L. 108-415 (118 Stat. 2337).

Lame-duck sessions have been used in recent years for various purposes, including efforts to bring action on regular appropriations acts for a fiscal year to a close. In addition to action on appropriations measures, lame-duck sessions have been used for such matters as the consideration of authorization measures for the Department of Defense and intelligence activities, the finalization of a measure establishing the Department of Homeland Security, and the impeachment proceedings against President Bill Clinton by the House.

Seventeen lame-duck sessions occurred between 1935 and 2008.[4] Ten of the 17 lame-duck sessions occurred during the half-century covering the decades of the 1940s through the 1980s, an average of one every five years.

The use of such sessions, however, has become more common in recent years, occurring about twice as frequently. The remaining seven lame-duck sessions, which occurred in 1994, 1998, 2000, 2002, 2004, 2006, and 2008, covered a span of eight Congresses. As **Table 1** shows, lame-duck sessions during this period occurred whether party control of the federal government was unified (i.e., the same party controlled the presidency and both chambers of Congress, as in 1994, 2004, and 2006) or divided. Further, lame-duck sessions occurred in presidential election years (2000, 2004, and 2008) as well as non-presidential election years.

OVERVIEW OF ACTION ON APPROPRIATIONS ACTS BEFORE, DURING, AND AFTER LAME-DUCK SESSIONS

In recent years, covering calendar years 1994 through 2008, lame-duck sessions have in some instances afforded Congress an opportunity to complete action on regular appropriations acts for a fiscal year. In other instances, lame-duck sessions played little or no role in this regard, as action on regular appropriations acts was completed well before or after a lame-duck session. A total of 88 regular appropriations acts were enacted into law for the fiscal years that coincided with lame-duck sessions, including 32 that were enacted separately and 56 that were included in omnibus measures.

In addition, a total of 43 continuing appropriations acts were enacted into law during this period. Like regular appropriations acts, the continuing appropriations acts were an important element in some, but not all, of the lame-duck sessions.

The two types of annual appropriations acts, regular appropriations acts (including omnibus measures) and continuing appropriations acts, are discussed separately below.

Regular Appropriations Acts

The variation regarding the role of lame-duck sessions in the consideration of regular appropriations acts is shown in **Figure 1** and **Table 2**. As the figure shows, all of the regular appropriations acts for a fiscal year were enacted into law before, during, or after the seven most recent lame-duck sessions held since 1994. During the 109th Congress, covering 2005 and 2006, the number of regular appropriations acts was reduced from 13 to 11 due to reorganization of the House and Senate Appropriations Committees.[5] With respect to 2006, two of the 11 regular appropriations acts (for FY2007) were enacted into law before the lame-duck session; the rest were funded by a continuing resolution for the entire fiscal year. At the beginning of the 110th Congress, a further reorganization of the appropriations subcommittees, which resulted in an increase in the number of annual appropriations acts to 12, took effect.[6] For FY2009, three appropriations acts, which were funded as part of a full-year continuing resolution, were completed before the lame-duck session began; the remaining nine appropriations acts were enacted via an omnibus appropriations act at the beginning of the 111th Congress.

In total, 45 of the 88 regular appropriations acts were enacted into law before the beginning of the applicable lame-duck session, 14 were enacted during a lame-duck session, and 29 were enacted afterwards.[7]

The occurrence of lame-duck sessions in 1994, 1998, and 2008 was not a factor in congressional action on annual appropriations acts. In 1994, all of the 13 regular appropriations acts for FY1995 were enacted into law before the beginning of the fiscal year. In 1998, one of the FY1999 regular appropriations acts was enacted before the start of the fiscal year, and the remaining 12 acts were enacted by October 21, nearly two months before the lame-duck session began on December 17. In 2008, work on three out of the 12 regular appropriations acts was completed before the end of September. The remaining nine acts were not considered until the beginning of the 111th Congress, where they were combined into an omnibus appropriations act and enacted into law on March 11, 2009.

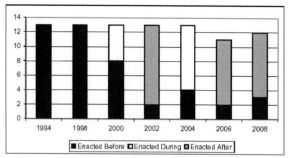

Source: Prepared by the Congressional Research Service.
Note: Four of the five regular appropriations acts for FY2001 considered during the lame-duck session in 2000 were signed into law six days after the sessions ended, but are considered for purposes of this memorandum as having been enacted during the lame-duck session.

Figure 1. Regular Appropriations Acts Enacted Before, During, and After Lame-Duck Sessions: 1994-2008.

Table 2. Enactment of Regular Appropriations Acts into Law Before, During, and After Lame-Duck Sessions: 1994-2008

Calendar Year	Number of Regular Appropriations Acts Enacted Into Law:			
	Before Lame-Duck Session	During Lame-Duck Session	After Lame-Duck Session	Total
1994	13	0	0	13
1998	13	0	0	13
2000	8	5	0	13
2002	2	0	11	13
2004	4	9	0	13
2006	2	0	9	11
2008	3	0	9	12
Total	**45**	**14**	**29**	**67**

Source: Prepared by the Congressional Research Service.
Note: Four of the five regular appropriations acts for FY2001 considered during the lame-duck session in 2000 were signed into law six days after the sessions ended, but are considered for purposes of this memorandum as having been enacted during the lame-duck session.

The consideration of annual appropriations acts was an important element in two lame-duck sessions. In 2000, eight regular appropriations acts were enacted before the lame-duck session, but the remaining five were enacted during (or immediately after) the session. In 2004, four regular appropriations acts were enacted before the lame-duck session, but the remaining nine were enacted during the session.

Finally, different patterns prevailed in the other two lame-duck sessions, held in 2002 and 2006, but the sessions again were not an important factor with respect to completing action on the regular appropriations acts. In each year, two of the regular appropriations acts (for FY2003 and FY2007, respectively) had been enacted into law before the lame-duck session began, but final action on the remaining acts was not completed until February of the following session.

The remaining 11 regular appropriations acts for FY2003 were incorporated into an omnibus appropriations measure, the Consolidated Appropriations Resolution for FY2003 (P.L. 108-7 ; February 20, 2003).

None of the remaining nine regular appropriations acts for FY2007 were enacted; instead, full-year funding was provided by a continuing resolution, the Revised Continuing Appropriations Resolution for FY2007 (P.L. 110-5; February 15, 2007).

Continuing Appropriations Acts

Continuing appropriations acts, commonly known as *continuing resolutions*, have been an integral component of the annual appropriations process for decades. Whenever action on one or more of the regular appropriations acts for a fiscal year is incomplete after the fiscal year has begun, continuing appropriations acts are used to provide stop-gap funding, thereby avoiding disruption in agency operations. One issue that arises under these circumstances is how continuing appropriations acts will be used to resolve any funding impasses and the appropriate duration of any period for their use.[8]

Continuing resolutions may have a relatively short duration in the expectation that action on the regular appropriations acts will be concluded within several days or weeks. In this case, multiple, short-term continuing resolutions often are used to "buy time" for ongoing negotiations on regular appropriations acts while maintaining incentives to complete the negotiations.

Table 3. Enactment of Continuing Appropriations Acts into Law Before, During, and After Lame-Duck Sessions: 1994-2008

Calendar Year	Number of Continuing Appropriations Acts Enacted Into Law:			
	Before Lame-Duck Session	During Lame-Duck Session	After Lame-Duck Session	Total
1994	0	0	0	0
1998	6	0	0	6
2000	15	6	0	21
2002	4	1	3	8
2004	1	2	0	3
2006	1	2	1	4
2008	1	0	0	1
Total	28	11	4	43

Source: Prepared by the Congressional Research Service.

Notes: In 2002, the continuing appropriations act for FY2003 considered during the lame-duck session was enacted into law on November 23, the day after the session ended. For purposes of this memorandum, the continuing appropriations act is considered to have been enacted during the lame-duck session.

Alternatively, continuing resolutions may have a longer duration to postpone final action on appropriations decisions until after elections or into the beginning of the next congressional session. Finally, a continuing resolution may provide funding for the remainder of the fiscal year.

Continuing appropriations acts have been an important element of action on annual appropriations measures before, during, and after some of the six lame-duck sessions held during the 1994-2008 period, but not others (see **Table 3**). A total of 43 continuing appropriations acts were enacted into law during this period.

In total, 28 of the 43 continuing appropriations acts were enacted into law before the beginning of the applicable lame-duck session, 11 were enacted during the lame-duck session, and four were enacted afterwards.[9]

In 1994, when all of the regular appropriations acts (for FY1995) were enacted into law in a timely manner, no continuing appropriations acts were needed. In 1998, when all of the regular appropriations acts (for FY1999) were enacted before the lame-duck session began (but not before the beginning of the fiscal year), six continuing appropriations acts were enacted to provide funding through the first three weeks of the fiscal year; none were needed afterwards, including during the lame-duck session. In 2008, a single continuing resolution was enacted before the fiscal year began that contained three regular appropriations acts and extended funding for the remaining FY2009 appropriations acts through March 6, 2009.

Circumstances were different with respect to the other four lame-duck sessions. In 2000, six continuing appropriations acts for FY2001 were enacted into law during the lame-duck session (15 had been enacted before the session began); in 2004, two continuing appropriations acts for FY2005 were enacted during the lame-duck session (one had been enacted beforehand). No continuing appropriations acts were needed, however, after the lame-duck sessions ended. In each year, a continuing appropriations act was enacted before the lame-duck session ended that extended stop-gap funding for five or six days, allowing sufficient time for the remaining regular appropriations acts to be enacted into law.

Finally, in the case of the two remaining lame-duck sessions, held in 2002 and 2006, continuing appropriations acts were needed both during and after the sessions. In 2002, one continuing appropriations act for FY2003 was enacted during the lame-duck session (four had been enacted before the session began); in 2006, two continuing appropriations acts for FY2007 were enacted during the lame-duck session (one had been enacted beforehand). For FY2003, three additional continuing appropriations acts were enacted into law early in the 2003 session before action was concluded with the enactment of an omnibus measure on February 20. For FY2007, action was concluded early in the 2007 session with the enactment of a full-year continuing resolution on February 15.

SUMMARY OF ACTION ON APPROPRIATIONS ACTS IN LAME-DUCK SESSIONS HELD IN 1994-2008

A brief summary of action on the annual appropriations acts considered during each of the five lame-duck sessions that occurred during the period from 1994 through 2008 is provided in this section and in **Table 4**, at the end of the report.

1994 and 1998 Lame-Duck Sessions

In 1994, a lame-duck session was held on November 29-December 1. All 13 of the regular appropriations acts for FY1995 were enacted into law prior to the start of the fiscal year on October 1, before the lame-duck session began; all were enacted separately. No continuing appropriations acts were needed.

In 1998, a lame-duck session was held on December 17-19. All 13 of the regular appropriations acts for FY1999 were enacted into law prior to the lame-duck session, five separately and eight in an omnibus measure, the Omnibus Consolidated and Emergency Supplemental Appropriations Act for FY1999 (P.L. 105-277; October 21, 2008). Six continuing appropriations acts were enacted to provide stop-gap funding through October 21.

Over the three days of the 1998 lame-duck session, the House considered and passed a resolution of impeachment against President Bill Clinton; the Senate was not in session.

No lame-duck session was held in the intervening election year, 1996.

2000 Lame-Duck Session

In 2000, a lame-duck session was held from November 13-December 15.

Eight of the 13 regular appropriations acts for FY2001 were enacted into law prior to the lame-duck session, six separately and two as part of an omnibus measure, the VA-HUD Appropriations Act for 2001 (P.L. 106-377; October 27, 2000), which also included funding for the Energy-Water Development Appropriations Act for FY2001.

The remaining five regular appropriations acts for FY2001were considered and enacted into law during the lame-duck session.[10] An omnibus measure, the Consolidated Appropriations Act for FY2001 (P.L. 106-554; December 21, 2000), covered the following three regular appropriations acts: (1) Labor-HHS-Education, (2) Legislative Branch, and (3) Treasury-Postal Service. The District of Columbia Appropriations Act for FY2001 (P.L. 106-522; November 22, 2000) and the Commerce-Justice-State Appropriations Act for FY2001 (P.L. 106-553; December 21, 2000) were enacted separately.

Fifteen continuing appropriations acts were enacted into law before the lame-duck session began. Six continuing appropriations acts were enacted into law during the lame-duck session.

2002 Lame-Duck Session

A lame-duck session was held on November 7-22, 2002. No regular appropriations acts were considered during the session.

Two of the regular appropriations acts for FY2003 were enacted into law before the lame-duck session began—the Defense Appropriations Act (P.L. 107-248) and the Military Construction Appropriations Act (P.L. 107-249); they both became law on October 23, 2002.

All of the remaining 11 regular appropriations acts for FY2003 were enacted into law early in the next Congress as a single measure, the Consolidated Appropriations Resolution for FY2003 (P.L. 108-7; February 20, 2003), many weeks after the lame-duck session had ended.

Four continuing appropriations act for FY2003 were enacted into law before the lame-duck session began. One further continuing appropriations act for the fiscal year was considered and enacted into law during the lame-duck session (P.L. 107-294; November 23, 2002).[11] Three more continuing appropriations acts were enacted early in the next Congress.

2004 Lame-Duck Session

The lame-duck session for 2004 was held on November 16-December 8.

Four of the 13 regular appropriations acts for FY2005 were enacted into law before the lame-duck session began (the Defense, District of Columbia, Homeland Security, and Military Construction Appropriations Acts); all were enacted separately.

The remaining nine regular appropriations acts for FY2005 were considered and enacted into law during the lame-duck session as part of an omnibus measure, the Consolidated Appropriations Act for FY2005 (P.L. 108-447; December 8, 2004).

One continuing appropriations act was enacted into law before the lame-duck session began. Two further continuing appropriations act for FY2005 were considered and enacted into law during the lame-duck session, P.L. 108-416 (November 21, 2004) and P.L. 108-434 (December 3, 2004).

2006 Lame-Duck Session

The lame-duck session for 2006 was held on November 13-December 9.

Two of the 11 regular appropriations acts for FY2007 were separately enacted before the lame-duck session began. The Defense Appropriations Act (P.L. 109-289) and the Homeland Security Appropriations Act (P.L. 109-295) were signed into law on September 29 and October 4, respectively. The nine other appropriations acts were extended through November 17 via a continuing resolution enacted on September 29 (P.L. 109-289).

Although a number of the remaining appropriations acts were considered by both the House and the Senate prior to the pre election recess[12], the only act to be considered by either chamber during the lame-duck session was H.R. 5385, the Military Construction, Military Quality of Life, and Veterans Affairs Appropriations Act, which was considered by the Senate and passed on November 14. Action on the nine regular appropriations acts was completed via a full-year continuing resolution (H.J.Res. 20) that was signed into law on February 15, 2007 (P.L. 110-5).

At the beginning of the lame-duck session, a second continuing resolution for FY2007 was enacted (P.L. 109-369) to provide appropriations through December 8. When it become apparent that action on regular appropriations would not be completed, a third continuing resolution was enacted (P.L. 109-383) that extended appropriations through February 15, 2007.

2008 Lame-Duck Session

The lame-duck session for 2008 was held on November 19-January 3. No regular appropriations acts were considered during the session.

Three of the 12 regular appropriations acts for FY2009 (Defense, Homeland Security, and Military Construction/Veteran's Affairs) were enacted before the lame-duck session via the Consolidated Security, Disaster Assistance, and Continuing Appropriations resolution, which became law on September 30 (P.L. 110-329). This continuing resolution extended funding for the nine remaining appropriations acts through March 6, 2009.

No action on appropriations was undertaken during the 2008 lame-duck session. The remaining appropriations acts were consolidated in the early days of the 111th Congress into the Omnibus Appropriations Act, 2009, which was signed by the President on March 11, 2009 (P.L. 111-8).

Table 4. Annual Appropriations Acts Enacted into Law During Lame-Duck Sessions: 1994-2008

Dates of Lame-Duck Session[a]	Appropriations Acts Enacted Into Law During the Lame-Duck Session	Commentary
103rd Congress		
1994 November 29- December 1	[none]	All 13 of the regular appropriations acts for FY1995 were enacted into law prior to the start of the fiscal year on October 1, before the lame-duck session; all were enacted separately.
104th Congress		
1996 [no lame-duck session held]	[none]	All 13 of the regular appropriations acts for FY1997 were enacted into law prior to the start of the fiscal year on October 1. Seven of the measures were enacted separately, and six were incorporated into an omnibus measure, the Omnibus Consolidated Appropriations Act for FY1997 (P.L. 104-208, September 30; 1996).
105th Congress		
1998 December 17- December 19	[none]	All 13 of the regular appropriations acts for FY1999 were enacted into law prior to the lame-duck session, five separately and eight in an omnibus measure, the Omnibus Consolidated and Emergency Supplemental Appropriations Act for FY1999 (P.L. 105-277; October 21, 2008). Over three days, the House considered and passed a resolution of impeachment against President Bill Clinton; the Senate was not in session.
106th Congress		
2000 November 13- December 15	Regular Appropriations Acts	Regular Appropriations Acts. Eight of the 13 regular appropriations acts for FY2001 were enacted into law prior to the lame-duck session, six separately and two as part of an omnibus measure, the VA-HUD Appropriations Act for 2001 (P.L. 106-377, October 27, 2000), which also included funding for the Energy-Water Development Appropriations Act for FY2001.

Table 4. (Continued)

Dates of Lame-Duck Session[a]	Appropriations Acts Enacted Into Law During the Lame-Duck Session	Commentary
	• P.L. 106-522, District of Columbia Approp-riations Act for FY2001 (November 22, 2000)	
	• P.L. 106-553, Commerce Justice State appro-priations Act for FY2001 (December 21, 2000)	The remaining five regular appropriations acts for FY2001 were considered and enacted into law during (or immediately after) the lame-duck session.[b] An omnibus measure, the Consolidated Appropriations Act for FY2001 (P.L. 106-554), covered the following three regular appropriations acts: (1) Labor-HHS-Education, (2) Legislative Branch, and (3) Treasury-Postal Service. The District of Columbia Appropriations Act for FY2001 (P.L. 106-522) and the Commerce-Justice-State Appropriations Act for FY2001 (P.L. 106-553) were enacted separately.
	• P.L. 106-554, Consolidated Appropriations Act For FY2001 (December 21, 2000)	
	Continuing Appropriations Acts	**Continuing Appropriations Acts.** Fifteen continuing appropriations acts were enacted into law before the lame-duck session began.
	• P.L. 106-520, Further Continuing Appropria-tions Act for FY2001 (November 15, 2000)	Six further continuing appropriations acts were considered and enacted during the lame-duck session.
	• P.L. 106-537, Further Continuing Appropria-tions Act for FY2001 (December 5, 2000)	

Table 4. (Continued)

Dates of Lame-Duck Session[a]	Appropriations Acts Enacted Into Law During the Lame-Duck Session	Commentary
	• P.L. 106-539, Further Continuing Appropria-tions Act for FY2001 (December 7, 2000)	
	• P.L. 106-540, Further Continuing Appropria-tions Act for FY2001 (December 8, 2000)	
	• P.L. 106-542, Further Continuing Appropria-tions Act for FY2001 (December 11, 2000)	
	• P.L. 106-543, Further Continuing Appropria-tions Act for FY2001 (December 15, 2000)	
107th Congress		
2002 November 7 - November 22	**Regular Appropriations Acts** [none]	**Regular Appropriations Acts.** Two of the 13 regular appropriations acts for FY2003 were enacted into law before the lame-duck session began (the Defense and Military Construction Appropriations Acts).
		All of the remaining 11 regular appropriations acts for FY2003 were considered and enacted into law early in the next Congress as an omnibus measure, the Con-solidated Appropriations Resolution for FY2003 (P.L. 108-7; February 20, 2003).
	Continuing Appropriations Acts	**Continuing Appropriations Acts.** Four continuing appropriations acts were enacted into law before the lame- duck session began.
	• P.L. 107-294, Further Continuing Appropria-tions Act for FY2003 (November 23, 2002)	One further continuing appropriations act for FY2003 was considered and enacted into law during the lame-duck session (P.L. 107-294).[c] Three more continuing appropriations acts were enacted early in the next Congress.

Table 4. (Continued)

Dates of Lame-Duck Session[a]	Appropriations Acts Enacted Into Law During the Lame-Duck Session	Commentary
108th Congress		
2004 November 16-December 8	**Regular Appropriations Acts** • P.L. 108-447, Consolidated Appropriations Act for FY2005 (December 8, 2004)	Regular Appropriations Acts. Four of the 13 regular appropriations acts for FY2005 were enacted into law before the lame-duck session began (the Defense, District of Columbia, Homeland Security, and Military Construction Appropriations Acts); all were enacted separately.
		The remaining nine regular appropriations acts for FY2005 were considered and enacted into law during the lame-duck session as part of an omnibus measure, the Consolidated Appropriations Act for FY2005 (P.L. 108- 447).
	Continuing Appropriations Acts	**Continuing Appropriations Acts.** One continuing appropriations act was enacted into law before the lame- duck session began.
	• P.L. 108-416, Further Continuing Appropria-tions Act for FY2005 (November 21, 2004)	Two further continuing appropriations act for FY2005 were considered and enacted into law during the lame- duck session (P.L. 108-416 and 108-434).
	• P.L. 108-434, Further Continuing Appropria-tions Act for FY2005 (December 3, 2004)	
109th Congress		
2006 November 9- December 9	**Regular Appropriations Acts** [none]	**Regular Appropriations Acts.** Two of the 11[d] regular appropriations acts for FY2007 were enacted into law before the lame-duck session began (the Defense and Homeland Security Appropriations Acts).

Table 4. (Continued)

Dates of Lame-Duck Session[a]	Appropriations Acts Enacted Into Law During the Lame-Duck Session	Commentary
		None of the remaining nine regular appropriations acts for FY2007 were enacted into law during (or after) the lame-duck session. Funding for the rest of the fiscal year for all of the remaining regular appropriations acts was provided early in the 110th Congress in a full-year continuing resolution, the Revised Continuing Appropriations Resolution for FY2007 (P.L. 110-5; February 15, 2007).
		During the lame-duck session, the Senate considered and passed H.R. 5385, the Military Construction, Military Quality of Life, and Veterans Affairs Appropriations Act, but the two chambers did not take any conference action on the bill.
	Continuing Appropriations Acts	**Continuing Appropriations Acts.** One continuing appropriations act was enacted into law before the lame- duck session began.
	• P.L. 109-369, Further Continuing Appropria-tions Act for FY2007 (November 17, 2006)	Two further continuing appropriations act for FY2007 were considered and enacted into law during the lame- duck session, (P.L. 109-369 and P.L. 109-383).
	• P.L. 109-383, Further Continuing Appropria-tions Act for FY2007 (December 9, 2004)	
110th Congress		
2008 November 19- January 3	**Regular Appropriations Acts** [none]	**Regular Appropriations Acts.** Three of the 12[d] regular appropriations acts for FY2009 were enacted into law before the lame-duck session began (the Defense, Homeland Security, and Military Construction/ Veteran's Affairs Appropriations Acts).
		The remaining nine regular appropriations acts for FY2009 were considered and enacted into law early in the next Congress via the Omnibus

Table 4. (Continued)

	Appropriations Act for FY2009 (P.L. 111-8; March 11, 2009).	
Dates of Lame-Duck Session[a]	**Appropriations Acts Enacted Into Law During the Lame-Duck Session**	**Commentary**
	Continuing Appropriations Acts [none]	Continuing Appropriations Acts. One continuing appropriations act was enacted into law before the lame-duck session began that extended appropriations through March 6, 2009 (P.L. 110-329).

Sources: Prepared by the Congressional Research Service from information provided in the Legislative Information System and the *Status Table of Appropriations* for various fiscal years at the CRS website (*http://www.crs.gov/products/appropriations/approver .shtml*).

a. The starting and ending dates refer to the first date and the last date that the House, the Senate, or both were in session after election day (the Tuesday after the first Monday in November). In 2002, the House and Senate stayed in session, rather than adjourning prior to the election and then reconvening; November 7 was the first day of session after election day, which was November 5 that year. In 2006, the Senate adjourned sine die after the House, but not until after 4:00 in the morning on December 9.

b. In 2000, the House and Senate completed action on five regular appropriations acts for FY2001 during the lame-duck session, but four of them were signed into law on December 21, six days after the session had ended. For purposes of this memorandum, all five acts are regarded as having been enacted during the lame-duck session.

c. In 2002, the continuing appropriations act for FY2003 considered during the lame-duck session was enacted into law on November 23, the day after the session ended. For purposes of this memorandum, the continuing appropriations act is considered to have been enacted during the lame-duck session.

d. The number of regular appropriations acts was changed from 13 to 11 during the 109th Congress as a result of reorganization of the House and Senate Appropriations Committees. This number was again changed from 11 to 12 in the 110th Congress due to the further reorganization of the Appropriations Committees that occurred in both chambers. For further information, see CRS Report RL31572, *Appropriations Subcommittee Structure: History of Changes from 1920-2007*, by James V. Saturno.

Acknowledgments

The original version of this report was written by Robert Keith, formerly a Specialist in American National Government at CRS. The listed author has revised and updated this report and is available to respond to inquiries on the subject.

End Notes

[1] Regular appropriations acts may be enacted as freestanding measures or as part of an omnibus appropriations act. For additional information on the latter, see CRS Report RL32473, *Omnibus Appropriations Acts: Overview of Recent Practices*, by Jessica Tollestrup.

[2] Section 2 of the 20th Amendment states: "The Congress shall assemble at least once in every year, and such meeting shall begin at noon on the 3d day of January, unless they shall by law appoint a different day." See "Constitution Annotated" on the CRS website at http://www.crs.gov/products/conan/WC01001.shtml.

[3] CRS Report RL33677, *Lame Duck Sessions of Congress, 1935-2008 (74th-110th Congresses)*, by Richard S. Beth.

[4] CRS Report RL33677, *Lame Duck Sessions of Congress, 1935-2008 (74th-110th Congresses)*, by Richard S. Beth, ibid., identifies 17 lame-duck sessions between 1935 and 2008 (see **Table 1**). According to the report, "[t]he possibility of a lame duck session of Congress in the modern sense began in 1935, when the 20th Amendment to the Constitution took effect" (p. 1).

[5] Although initial consideration of appropriations legislation in the two chambers differed in both the number and substance of the appropriations acts, the final acts that were agreed to numbered 11. For further information on this change, see CRS Report RL31572, *Appropriations Subcommittee Structure: History of Changes from 1920-2007*, by James V. Saturno.

[6] Ibid.

[7] In 2000, the House and Senate completed action on five regular appropriations acts for FY2001 during the lame-duck session, but four of them were signed into law on December 21, six days after the session had ended. For purposes of this memorandum, all five acts are regarded as having been enacted during the lame-duck session.

[8] For a more detailed discussion of this topic, see CRS Report RL32614, *Duration of Continuing Resolutions in Recent Years*, by Jessica Tollestrup.

[9] In 2002, the continuing appropriations act for FY2003 considered during the lame-duck session was enacted into law on November 23, the day after the session ended. For purposes of this memorandum, the continuing appropriations act is considered to have been enacted during the lame-duck session.

[10] The House and Senate completed action on five regular appropriations acts for FY2001 during the lame-duck session, but four of them were signed into law on December 21, 2000, six days after the session had ended. For purposes of this memorandum, all five acts are regarded as having been enacted during the lame-duck session.

[11] The continuing appropriations act was considered during the lame-duck session but was enacted into law on November 23, the day after the session ended. For purposes of this memorandum, the continuing appropriations act is considered to have been enacted during the lame-duck session.

[12] The House recessed on October 3, 2008. The Senate held *pro forma* sessions through the beginning of the lame-duck session on November 19, 2008.

In: Overview of Congressional Appropriations   ISBN: 978-1-61209-849-4
Editors: J.M. Stewart, D.M. Allworth   © 2011 Nova Science Publishers, Inc.

Chapter 5

HOUSE OFFSET AMENDMENTS TO APPROPRIATIONS BILLS: PROCEDURAL CONSIDERATIONS

Sandy Streeter

SUMMARY

One of the most common methods for changing spending priorities in appropriations bills on the House floor is through *offset amendments*. House offset amendments generally change spending priorities in a pending appropriations measure by increasing spending for certain activities (or creating spending for new activities not included in the bill) and offsetting the increase with funding decreases in other activities in the bill. Offset amendments are needed to avoid the Congressional Budget Act 302(f) and 311(a) points of order enforcing certain spending ceilings.

There are two types of House offset amendments considered in the Committee of the Whole House on the State of the Union (Committee of the Whole): clause 2(f) and reachback (or fetchback) amendments. As provided under House Rule XXI, *clause 2(f) offset amendments* consist of two or more amendments considered together (or en bloc) that would change amounts by directly adding text or changing text in the body of the bill. Taken as a whole the amendment does not increase the amount of funding in the pending bill. Such amendments (1) must provide offsets in both new budget authority and outlays, (2) may contain certain unauthorized appropriations, (3) cannot add new appropriations or spending set asides, and (4) must not contain legislation.

Reachback offset amendments are generally offered at the end of the bill and change funding amounts in the pending bill by reference. These amendments (1) must provide offsets in new budget authority, but not necessarily offsets, (2) cannot include unauthorized appropriations, (3) may add new appropriations (and spending set asides), (4) cannot contain legislation, and (5) may provide across-the-board spending reductions as offsets.

Parliamentary rules governing consideration of offset amendments may be suspended or waived, typically by House adoption of a special rule, but also by unanimous consent.

The significant advantages of clause 2(f) amendments over reachback amendments are that clause 2(f) amendments may contain certain unauthorized appropriations and are typically considered before reachback amendments, sometimes limiting offset opportunities for reachback amendments. The main advantages of reachback amendments are they may add new appropriations and include across-the-board spending reductions.

INTRODUCTION

One of the most common methods for redistributing spending priorities in appropriations bills on the House floor is through offset amendments. House *offset amendments* generally change spending priorities in a pending appropriations measure by increasing spending for certain activities (or creating spending for new activities not included in the bill) and offsetting the increase(s) by decreasing or striking funding for other activities in the bill. For example, an amendment increasing funding for one agency funded in the bill by $3 million and decreasing funding for another agency by the same amount in the same bill would be an offset amendment.

These amendments may transfer funds between two activities or among several activities. In addition, certain offset amendments may reduce funding with across-the-board spending reductions.

Representatives use offset amendments for a variety of reasons. Three are to (1) ensure that proposals increasing funding for certain activities in an appropriations bill do not violate parliamentary rules enforcing certain spending ceilings;[1] (2) garner support for efforts to reduce funding for certain activities by transferring those funds to popular programs; and (3) provide a focal point for discussion of a particular issue.

This report is an introduction to selected House rules and practices governing the consideration of offset amendments to appropriations measures considered in the Committee of the Whole House on the State of the Union (or Committee of the Whole).[2] Issues analyzed below are spending ceilings and offset amendments; two types of offset amendments, clause 2(f) and reachback (or fetchback) offset amendments, including procedural factors regarding each; and mechanisms waiving House rules. The report concludes with highlights on the procedural advantages of each offset amendment type.

SPENDING CEILINGS AND OFFSET AMENDMENTS

Offset amendments enable members to propose amendments including certain funding increases to appropriations measures that are subject to enforceable spending ceilings.

General Rules

Each spring, Congress considers an annual budget resolution, which is under the jurisdiction of the House and Senate Budget Committees. This resolution establishes, in part, total new budget authority[3] and outlay ceilings for federal government activities for the upcoming fiscal year. Once these figures are finalized, the new budget authority and outlays are allocated among the House committees with jurisdiction over spending, and each committee is given specific spending ceilings (referred to as the *302(a) allocations*).[4] The House Appropriations Committee receives separate allocations for discretionary and mandatory spending;[5] and, in turn, subdivides their 302(a) allocations among their 12 appropriations subcommittee,[6] providing each subcommittee with their spending ceilings (*302(b) allocations*). In the case of the appropriations committee, these allocations are only established for the upcoming fiscal year, because appropriations measures are annual.

Two Congressional Budget Act points of order, 302(f) and 311(a) points of order, enforce selected spending ceilings.[7] First, the 302(f) point of order prohibits, in part, floor consideration of any appropriations measure and related amendments[8] providing new budget authority for the upcoming fiscal year that would cause the applicable 3 02(a) or 302(b) allocations of new budget authority for that fiscal year to be exceeded. In effect, the application of this point of order on appropriations legislation is generally limited to discretionary spending. If, for example, the 302(b) allocation in new discretionary budget authority a fiscal year is $24 billion and the reported bill would provide the same amount for the same fiscal year, any amendment proposing an increase in new discretionary budget authority for activities in the bill (or creating new discretionary budget authority) would violate the 3 02(f) point of order. An offset amendment, however, that also includes a commensurate decrease in new discretionary budget authority for activities in the bill would not violate the rule.

The second rule, the 311(a) point of order, prohibits, in part, floor consideration of any appropriations measure and related amendments providing new budget authority for the upcoming fiscal year that would cause the applicable total budget authority and outlay ceilings in the budget resolution for that fiscal year to be exceeded.[9] As the amounts of all the spending measures considered in the House accumulate, they could potentially reach or exceed these ceilings. This point of order would typically affect the last spending bills to be considered, such as supplemental appropriations measures or the last regular appropriations bills.

If a Representative raises a point of order that an amendment violates either rule and the presiding officer sustains the point of order, the amendment falls.

Appropriations measures considered on the House floor are typically at or just below the level of the subcommittee's 302(b) allocation and, in some cases, the committee's 302(a) allocation and the total spending ceiling as well. As a result, amendments that would increase new budget authority in an appropriations measure must typically include offsets.

Appropriations Measures: Selected Content

The structure of appropriations measures has a direct impact on the form of offset amendments. Regular appropriations bills and supplementals generally include several lump-sum and line-item appropriations, so that adding a new appropriation or increasing funding for an appropriation in the bill typically requires an offset. The procedural necessity of an offset for a funding set asides within a lump-sum appropriation is dependent on the structure of the appropriation in the bill.

Lump-Sum and Line-Item Appropriations

Regular appropriations bills and supplemental appropriations measures generally contain numerous unnumbered paragraphs. Most paragraphs provide a lump-sum amount (usually an appropriation) for similar programs, projects, or activities, such paragraphs are referred to as *lump-sum appropriations*. A few paragraphs provide an appropriation for a single program or project, referred to as a *line item appropriation*.[10] Most appropriations correspond to a unique budget account.

The total net spending levels provided in an appropriations bill includes all lump-sum and line item appropriations, provisions cancelling previously enacted budget authority as well as other provisions affecting spending. Appropriations bills considered on the House floor are typically near or at the level of the subcommittee's 3 02(b) allocation. An amendment increasing a lump- sum appropriation or adding a new appropriation, therefore, could increase the amount of funding in the bill causing it to exceed this limit, so that it typically requires an offset.

Funding Set Asides

Within a lump-sum appropriation, separate amounts are sometimes included in the bill that set aside spending for specified programs, projects, or activities (for purposes of this report, they are referred to as *funding set asides*). Congressional earmarks (or congressionally directed spending items) included in appropriations bills are typically funding set asides.[11]

An amendment proposing to increase (or create) a funding set aside in a lump-sum appropriation that has been entirely set aside in the bill would procedurally require a commensurate offset. In the example below, the three set asides total $200,000,000, which is the total lump-sum amount.

An amendment proposing an increase in any of the three set asides that does not include an offset in one of the other set asides, would require an increase of the lump-sum amount.

> For necessary expenses, including salaries and related expenses, of the Executive Office for YYY, to implement program activities, $200,000,000, of which *$100,000,000* is for the yellow program, *$50,000,000* for the green program, and *$50,000,000* for the blue program.

By contrast, certain set aside amendments would not increase lump-sum amounts. If a bill contains a lump-sum amount with no set asides, for example, an amendment designating part (or all) of the funds for a particular purpose would not increase spending. In cases in which the lump- sum appropriation includes a set aside(s) that does not affect the entire amount, an amendment setting aside only the remaining funds or a portion of those funds would also not increase spending. If enacted, the effect of either case would be reductions in funding for activities that was not set aside in order to accommodate funding in the bill that was specified as set asides. To avoid such reductions, amendments may include offsets from other appropriations in the bill.

TYPES OF OFFSET AMENDMENTS

There are two types of offset amendments, clause 2(f) and reachback (or fetchback) amendments, available during consideration of regular and supplemental appropriations bills in the Committee of the Whole. Clause 2(f) refers to clause 2(f) of House Rule XXI, which establishes some of the parliamentary procedures governing the consideration of such amendments. [12]

Clause 2(f) Offset Amendments

Clause 2(f) offset amendments consist of two or more amendments considered together (or en bloc)[13] that would change amounts by directly adding text or changing text in the body of the bill; as opposed to reachback offset amendments, which are generally offered at the end of the bill, that change funding amounts by reference. The clause 2(f) offset amendment transfers funds among appropriations or activities in the pending bill and, taken as a whole, does not cause the bill to exceed the total new budget authority or outlay levels already provided in the bill. If the reported bill provides a total spending level(s) lower than the 302(a) and 302(b) ceilings, the sponsor of a clause 2(f) offset amendment can not use the difference. The member must provide a full offset to pay for the proposed increase. As noted above, however, appropriations bills considered on the House floor are typically at or just below the 302(b) allocations.

An example of a clause 2(f) offset amendment follows. This amendment would have decreased the lump-sum appropriation for the Bureau of the Census, Periodic Censuses and Programs account by $10 million; increased the lump-sum appropriation for the Office of Justice Programs, State and Local Law Enforcement Assistance account by $10 million; and increased a set aside within the latter appropriation for Southwest Border Prosecutor Initiative by the same amount.

> Page 6, line 23, after the dollar amount insert "
> (reduced by $10,000,000)."
> Page 42, line 8, after the dollar amount insert "
> (increased by $10,000,000)."
> Page 43, line 8, after the dollar amount insert "
> (increased by $10,000,000)."[14]

These offset amendments typically change a spending level by inserting after the amount a parenthetic increase or decrease (see example above). Under House rules, an amendment generally cannot amend text previously amended. [15] Changing a monetary figure by a parenthetic increase or decrease placed after the amount text, rather than changing the amount text, however, is allowed. [16]

Under House rules, clause 2(f) offset amendments must be offered when the first portion of the bill to be amended is pending, but the Committee of the Whole may waive this requirement by unanimous consent.[17] In Committee of the Whole, appropriations bills are generally read for amendment sequentially by paragraph. After the reading clerk reads or designates a paragraph, the presiding officer entertains points of order against that paragraph, and then members propose amendments to it. After the clerk has designated or begun reading the next paragraph, amendments to the former paragraph are not in order.[18]

Prior to consideration of a proposed clause 2(f) offset amendment, the Presiding Officer asks if any member wants to raise a point of order against any provision the en bloc amendment would change. If a point of order against such a provision is sustained, the provision is stricken from the bill and is no longer amendable. Therefore, the offset amendment would fall as well, unless appropriately modified or amended by unanimous consent.

Four additional procedural requirements regarding clause 2(f) offset amendments are discussed below. These amendments (1) must offset any increase in both budget authority and outlays; (2) may contain certain unauthorized appropriations; (3) cannot add new appropriations or funding set asides; and (4) cannot contain legislation.

Table 1. Distribution of Outlays (in Millions of Dollars)

Account	FY2009	FY2010	FY2011	FY2012	Total
Operating Expenses	18	2	—	—	20
Construction	2	2	8	8	20

Source: Table compiled by the Congressional Research Service.

Must Offset Both Budget Authority and Outlays

Under House Rule XXI, clause 2(f), any spending increases in a clause 2(f) offset amendment must be offset by commensurate reductions in both new budget authority and outlays. By contrast, the 302(f) point of order only enforces 302(a) and 302(b) allocations of new budget authority.[19] The spending increases and decreases contained in an offset amendment must be provided in the same fiscal year, the year of the pending appropriations bill.

Offset amendments providing equal increases and decreases in new budget authority might not produce equal amounts of outlays in the same fiscal year. The amount of resulting outlays may vary among different accounts, because the length of time needed to complete the activities funded may differ. It takes less time to purchase office supplies than to complete construction of an aircraft. For example, in **Table 1**, the distribution of outlays from $20 million in new budget authority varies between two accounts.

Based on historical spending practices, the Congressional Budget Office (CBO) each year estimates the speed at which outlays from each appropriation will occur, referred to as the *spendout rates* (or *outlay rates*). A spendout rate is the rate at which budget authority is expected to be spent (outlays) in a fiscal year.[20] In **Table 1**, the FY2009 spending rate for the operating expenses account is 90%, while the rate for the construction account is 10%.

The varying spendout rates of appropriations sometimes complicate efforts to increase budget authority. In **Table 2**, increasing FY2009 budget authority for an operating expenses account by $20 million produces $18 million in outlays. Decreasing a construction account by the same amount in budget authority, however, produces only $2 million in outlays. Under this scenario, reductions in three accounts produce the $18 million in outlays needed to fund the $20 million budget authority increase in operating expenses. By contrast, increasing the construction account by $20 million in budget authority would be easier since only $2 million in outlays would be required.

Table 2. Budget Authority, Spendout Rate, and Outlays (in Millions of Dollars)

Budget Authority	FY2009 Budget Authority	Spendout Rate for FY2009	FY2009 Outlays
Increase			
Operating Expenses	20	90%	18
Offsets			
Construction	20	10	2
Government Assistance Program	20	20	4
Security	20	60	12
Total	60		18

Source: Table compiled by the Congressional Research Service.

Representatives (or their staff) routinely ask CBO to estimate the budgetary impact of their clause 2(f) offset amendments. A CBO estimate is required because s while the Congressional Budget Act gives the authority for scoring amendments subject to the 302(f) and 311(a) points of order to the House Budget Committee, the committee relies on CBO's determinations.

Can Not Add New Appropriations or Funding Set Asides

Clause 2(f) offset amendments can only change dollar amounts in the bill. They cannot add a new lump-sum appropriation or set aside, even if the lump-sum or set aside does not violate other parliamentary rules.

May Not Contain Legislation

House Rule XXI, clause 2(b), prohibits legislation in committee-reported general appropriations measures and clause 2(c) prohibits legislation in amendments to those measures.[21] For purposes of this rule, *legislation* refers to any provision in an appropriations bill or related amendment that changes existing law, such as proposals amending or repealing existing law, or creating new law. The following are examples of legislative language: abolishing a department, agency, or program; providing, changing, limiting, or waiving an authorization; providing emergency designations for appropriations;[22] or increasing rescissions in the appropriations bill.[23]

May Contain Certain Unauthorized Appropriations

House Rule XXI, clause 2(a), generally prohibits unauthorized appropriations in certain committee-reported appropriations bills and amendments to such bills.[24] Certain amendments, such as clause 2(f) offset amendments, however, may increase the level of funding for certain unauthorized appropriations already in the bill.

Under clause 2(a), legislation must generally be enacted authorizing subsequent appropriations for a program (or an agency, account, project, or activity) before appropriations for that program can be considered on the House floor. An "[a]uthorization for a program may be derived from a specific law providing authority for that particular program or from a more general existing law— "organic law"—authorizing appropriations for such programs."[25]

The rule prohibits floor consideration of appropriations for a program whose authorization has expired or was never authorized, or whose budget authority exceeds the ceiling authorized. Appropriations violating these restrictions are *unauthorized appropriations*.[26] While this prohibition applies to *general appropriations bills*, regular appropriations bills and supplemental appropriations measures which provide funds for more than one purpose or agency; it does not apply to continuing resolutions.[27]

Appropriations bills frequently include unauthorized appropriations. Such appropriations are allowed to remain in an appropriations bill when the House adopts a special rule waiving points of order against the appropriation; or, less frequently, when no one raises a point of order against it.[28] Under House precedents, a germane amendment that merely perfects an unauthorized appropriation permitted to remain in the bill is allowed.[29] An example would be an amendment that would only increase the unauthorized amount and would do it by either amending the amount text or by inserting a parenthetical increase after the amount (such as an en bloc clause 2(f) offset amendment) would could be allowed. A scenario providing the stages of action:

1. An authorization act provided an authorization of appropriations of $2 million for program yellow through FY2008; as of the close of FY2008, the authorization had expired.
2. Subsequently, an FY2009 regular appropriations bill provides an unauthorized appropriation of $2 million for program yellow.
3. The House adopts a special rule waiving House Rule XXI, clause 2(a) against all provisions in the bill, allowing the above appropriation to remain.

4. A clause 2(f) offset amendment parenthetically increasing the unauthorized appropriation by $1 million for program yellow is allowed.

Although clause 2(f) offset amendments may increase unauthorized appropriations, they remain subject to the spending ceilings enforced by the 302(f) and 311(a) points of order as well as by House Rule XXI, clause 2(f).

A clause 2(f) amendment may not propose to increase an "authorized appropriation" in an appropriations bill beyond the authorized level. In the scenario above, for example, the authorization act included a $2 million authorization for FY2009 and the regular appropriations bill provided the full amount, an offset amendment increasing the amount by $1 million would be prohibited.

Exempt from a "Demand for a Division of the Question"

Under House Rule XXI, clause 2(f), these amendments are not subject to a "demand for a division of the question." That is, a member cannot demand separate consideration of two or more provisions in such en bloc amendments, instead the House considers the amendment as a whole.[30]

Reachback Offset Amendments

Reachback (or *fetchback*) *offset amendments* add a new section (or title), typically at the end of an appropriations measure, that reaches back to change amounts previously considered by reference.[31] For example, the following amendment would have inserted a new section at the end of the FY2008 Labor, Health and Human Services, and Education regular appropriations bill:

Title VI—Additional General Provisions

Sec. 601. The amounts otherwise provided by this Act are revised by reducing the amount made available for the "Department of Labor, Employment and Training Administration, Training and Employment Services", by increasing the amount made available for the "National Institutes of Health, National Cancer Institute", and by increasing the amount made available for the "National Institutes of Health, National Institute of Neurological Disorders and Stroke" by $49,000,000, $10,000,000, and $10,000,000, respectively.[32]

In contrast to clause 2(f) offset amendments, reachback amendments may increase spending provided in the bill as long as they do not violate sections 302(f) and 311(a) points of order. [33]

Reachback amendments

- must offset budget authority, may not necessarily have to offset outlays;
- may not include unauthorized appropriations;
- may add new lump-sum appropriations and set asides subject to certain restrictions;
- may not contain legislation;
- may provide across-the-board spending reductions as offsets; and
- must be drafted to avoid a demand for a division of the question.

Must Offset Budget Authority, May Not Necessarily Have To Offset Outlays

Both Congressional Budget Act points of order enforce new budget authority, but only the 311(a) point of order also enforces outlays. Of the three enforceable spending levels, the 302(b) new budget authority allocations are generally the more restrictive. Furthermore, only the last spending measures considered for a fiscal year, typically supplementals or last regular bills, are subject to the 311(a) point of order. For reachback amendments, budget authority offsets are generally the primary procedural concern.

Opponents of a reachback amendment may, however, raise the lack of outlay offsets as a concern for policy reasons. They might also argue that the resulting outlay increases might present a procedural problem for the bill in the Senate or in conference.[34]

In the case of reachback amendments that also provide sufficient new budget authority reductions to offset any outlay increases, Representatives (or their staff) routinely ask CBO to estimate the outlay effect of their amendments.[35]

The spending increases and decreases contained in an offset amendment must be provided in the same fiscal year, the year of the pending appropriations bill.

May Add New Appropriations (and Set asides)

Reachback amendments may contain new appropriations and set asides for certain activities not already included in the bill. Such new appropriations and set asides must be germane to the bill.

Under House Rule XVI, clause 7,[36] all amendments must be *germane* to the pending bill. That is, they may not add new subject matter to the bill. Reachback amendments offered at the end of the bill must be germane to the bill, while those offered at the end of a title must be germane to the title. Regular appropriations measures generally have broad subject matter, which may provide flexibility for reachback amendments.

May Not Contain Legislation

Reachback amendments may not change existing law.[37] As a result, amendments adding new set asides are often restricted by this prohibition.

One of the guiding principles in interpreting this prohibition is that an amendment designating funds may not interfere with an executive branch official's statutory authority, for example, they may not significantly alter the official's discretion. Such language changes existing law and is, therefore, prohibited. For example, if an authorization law provides an agency head with the authority to allocate funds within a particular lump-sum appropriation, an amendment proposing a new set aside would alter the agency head's authority and would be out of order.

Where a new set aside would violate the rules, an amendment sponsor frequently does not include the set aside in the amendment; instead, the sponsor discusses it during debate on the amendment. This approach is used to avoid the point of order against the amendment. During conference on the bill, the amendment sponsor may urge the conferees to include the set aside in the conference report or accompanying joint explanatory statement.

May Not Include Unauthorized Appropriations

Under House Rule XXI, clause 2(a), new appropriations and set asides included in amendments must be proposed for authorized purposes. All new set asides must also be proposed to authorized lump-sum appropriations.[38]

In contrast to clause 2(f) offset amendments, reachback amendments may not increase unauthorized appropriations permitted to remain in the bill because they do not change the text of the bill. The section added by a reachback amendment is considered adding a further unauthorized appropriation, as opposed to merely perfecting the text.[39]

Must Be Drafted to Avoid a "Demand for a Division of the Question"

Under House Rule XVI, clause 5,[40] a member may demand separate consideration of two or more individual portions of an amendment if each portion identified, when standing alone, is a separate, substantive proposition and is grammatically separate "... so that if one proposition is rejected a separate proposition will logically remain."

Because reachback amendments are potentially subject to a demand for a division of the question, if the presiding officer rules that an amendment is divisible, each divided portion of the amendment would considered separately and subject to separate debate and amendment, as well as a separate vote. members often demand a division of the question on an amendment in order to defeat one or more of the portions of an amendment. For example, a majority of members might be opposed to the portion of an offset amendment that decreases funds for a particular program. One of them might demand a division of question that, if granted, would allow a separate vote on the funding decrease portion of the amendment. Individual portions of the amendment may also be subject to the Congressional Budget Act points of order.

May Provide Across-the-Board Spending Reductions as Offsets

Reachback amendments may include as an offset across-the-board spending cuts, while clause 2(f) amendments may only directly change amounts in the bill.

PROCEDURAL CONSIDERATIONS

Parliamentary rules may be suspended or waived in order to consider offset amendments that violate these rules, typically by House adoption of a special rule. However, this approach has been used infrequently.

There are certain procedural advantages of clause 2(f) amendments over reachback amendments as well as vice versa.

Opportunities to Waive Parliamentary Rules

There are generally three limited opportunities to suspend or waive the rules governing consideration of an offset amendment: (1) if no one raises a point of order the rules would implicitly be waived; (2) if the House adopts a special rule explicitly waiving points of order against the amendment; or (3) if the House agrees by unanimous consent to waive the rules. Otherwise, if the presiding officer sustains a point of order against an amendment for violating the parliamentary rules previously discussed, the amendment falls.

First, House rules are not generally self-enforcing. A Representative must raise a point of order that an amendment violates a specific rule. If no one opposes an amendment, a point of order does not have to be raised.

Second, under current practice, the House Committee on Rules usually reports a special rule setting additional procedural parameters for the consideration of appropriations measures. The House typically adopts the special rule and then considers the particular appropriations measure pursuant to it, as well as any subsequent unanimous consent agreement.[41] If an offset amendment would violate one or more parliamentary rules, the sponsor may ask the Rules Committee to include a waiver protecting the amendment from the point(s) of order.

Although special rules generally do not provide special protection for offset amendments to regular appropriations bills, they have sometimes protected those to supplemental appropriations measures. The rationale for protecting clause 2(f) amendments is that the opportunity to offer offset amendments is otherwise extremely limited. The 302(f) point of order requires that funding increases and offsets are under the same subcommittee. Clause 2(f) amendments and generally reachback amendments must include offsets from the pending bill. Supplementals may not include funding for accounts in each subcommittee (or most subcommittees); furthermore, they often include a limited number of accounts under subcommittees included. As a result, there are relatively few offset opportunities.

Third, a member might ask to consider an amendment violating the rules by unanimous consent. A single member, however, can prevent such consideration by simply objecting to the unanimous consent request.

To attain their policy objectives, sponsors of controversial offset amendments generally select either a clause 2(f) or reachback amendment and work within the rules governing their consideration.

Selected Procedural Advantages of Clause 2(f) Amendments

May Include Unauthorized Appropriations

Appropriations bills typically include some unauthorized appropriations. Generally, the House Rules Committee reports a special rule adopted by the House, waiving the prohibition against unauthorized appropriations for most or all unauthorized appropriations in a reported bill. Clause 2(f) amendments can increase those unauthorized appropriations allowed to remain. Reachback amendments, however, can only increase authorized appropriations in the bill to their authorized level (if there is one).

In some cases, entire bills or significant portions of bills have consisted of unauthorized appropriations. As a result, reachback amendments could not increase those amounts. For example, many of the lump-sum appropriations provided in the committee-reported regular defense appropriations bills have typically been unauthorized because of the timing of consideration of the annual defense authorization bill. The House has adopted special rules regarding each bill waiving the application of House Rule XXI, clause 2. As a result, clause 2(f) amendments to those bills were in order, while reachback amendments were limited to the few, if any, authorized appropriations.

Considered Earlier

The timing of clause 2(f) amendments is sometimes an advantage over reachback amendments since clause 2(f) amendments are offered earlier in a bill's consideration. By the time reachback amendments are considered, there may be fewer politically appealing offset options available. Amendments, including clause 2(f) amendments may have already been adopted that reduced the account a reachback amendment sponsor selected for offsets. The account might be reduced so low that there is no support for further reductions.

Selected Procedural Advantages of Reachback Amendments

May Add New Lump-Sum Appropriations or Set asides

Reachback amendments may add new lump-sum appropriations and some set asides within certain restrictions, while clause 2(f) amendments are limited only to changing amounts already in the bill.

May Provide Across-the-Board Cuts in Spending

Reachback amendments may include as an offset an across-the-board spending cut, while clause 2(f) amendments may only directly change amounts in the bill.

May Exceed Bill's Total Spending Levels

Reachback amendments can exceed the bill's total spending level, while clause 2(f) amendments cannot. This advantage is limited, however, since most appropriations bills considered on the floor are either at or just below the subcommittee allocations.

May Not Necessarily Have to Offset Outlays

Another limited advantage of reachback amendments is that for most appropriations bills, reachback amendments must offset only new budget authority. Clause 2(f) amendments must offset both new budget authority and outlays. In practice, however, this advantage of reachback amendments over clause 2(f) amendments is limited because, in order to garner political support for reachback amendments, sponsors sometimes provide offsets in both budget authority and outlays.

Acknowledgments

The author is grateful to the following individuals for their advice: Ira Forstater, House Office of the Legislative Counsel; Thomas J. Wickham, House Office of the Parliamentarian; and James V. Saturno, Congressional Research Service.

End Notes

[1] See "Spending Ceilings and Offset Amendments" below.
[2] House Rule XVIII, clause 3, requires that appropriations measures be considered in the Committee of the Whole before the House votes on passage of the measures (see CRS Report 95-563, *The Legislative Process on the House Floor: An Introduction*, by Christopher M. Davis).
[3] *Budget authority* does not represent cash provided to or reserved for agencies, instead the term refers to authority provided by federal law to enter into contracts or other financial *obligations* that will result in immediate or future expenditures (or *outlays*) involving federal government funds. Most *appropriations* are a form of budget authority that also provide legal authority to make the subsequent payments from the Treasury.

[4] The Congressional Budget and Impoundment Control Act of 1974 (Congressional Budget Act (2 U.S.C. § 621 et seq.) established this process. The terms 3 02(a) and 302(b) allocations refer to sections 3 02(a) and 3 02(b) of the act.

[5] Congress divides spending into two categories: *discretionary* and *mandatory* (or *direct*) *spending*. Discretionary spending is controlled by annual appropriations acts, which are under the jurisdiction of the House and Senate Committees on Appropriations. Mandatory spending is controlled by legislative acts under the jurisdiction of the authorizing committees (principally, the House Committee on Ways and Means and Senate Committee on Finance). All discretionary spending and some mandatory spending are included in the annual appropriations measures. For more information, see CRS Report 97-684, *The Congressional Appropriations Process: An Introduction*, by Sandy Streeter.

[6] Each House appropriations subcommittee has jurisdiction over a single regular appropriations bill. There are three major types of appropriations measures: regular appropriations bills, supplemental appropriations measures (or supplementals), and continuing resolutions. Of the three types, *regular appropriations bills* generally provide most of the funding (either as separate acts or in omnibus acts). *Supplemental appropriations measures* (or supplementals) generally increase funding for selected activities previously funded in the regular bills, although recently supplementals have provided funds for the wars in Iraq and Afghanistan. *Continuing resolutions* extend funding for agencies, if any regular appropriations bill does not become law by the October 1 deadline. The House typically agrees to prohibit amendments to continuing resolutions.

[7] The 302(f) and 311(a) points of order refer to sections 302(f) and 311(a) of the Congressional Budget Act.

[8] Both the 302(f) and 311(a) rules also apply to conference reports to appropriations measures.

[9] This rule exempts, in part, appropriations measures and related amendments, that would not cause the 3 02(a) allocation to be exceeded, referred to as the *Fazio exception*.

[10] Each large agency, whether under a department or independent, are typically funded by several appropriations. All programs, projects, and activities under a small agency may be funded with a single lump-sum appropriation.

[11] For more information on congressional earmarks, see CRS Report RL34462, *House and Senate Procedural Rules Concerning Earmark Disclosure*, by Sandy Streeter.

[12] House Rule XXI, clause 2(f):During the reading of an appropriation bill for amendment in the Committee of the Whole House on the state of the Union [Committee of the Whole], it shall be in order to consider en bloc amendments proposing only to transfer appropriations among objects in the bill without increasing the levels of budget authority or outlays in the bill. When considered en bloc under this paragraph, such amendments may amend portions of the bill not yet read for amendment (following disposition of any points of order against such portions) and are not subject to a demand for division of the question in the House or in the Committee of the Whole.U.S. Congress, House, *Constitution, Jefferson's Manual, and Rules of the House of Representatives, 110th Congress* (or *House Manual*), 1 10th Cong., 2nd sess., H.Doc. 109-157 (Washington: GPO, 2007).

[13] Under the House Rule XXI, clause 2(f) amendments are allowed to be considered en bloc. Other amendments may generally not be considered en bloc unless by unanimous consent or pursuant to the terms of a special rule. U.S. Congress, House, *House Practice: A Guide to the Rules, Precedents, and Procedures of th House* (or *House Practice*), 108th Cong., 1st sess., prepared by Wm. Holmes Brown and Charles W. Johnson (Washington: GPO, 2003), chapter 2, section 30.

[14] Representative Capito, remarks in the House, *Congressional Record* (daily edition), vol. 153 (July 25, 2007), p. H8435. The amendment was offered to the FY2008 Commerce, Justice, and Science appropriations bill.

[15] *House Manual*, section 469.

[16] *House Practice*, chapter 2, section 42.

[17] That is, the amendment is allowed to be offered out of order if no Representative objects. The House could also adopt a special rule waiving the point of order. Prior to consideration of an appropriations bill, the House typically adopts a special rule setting procedures parameters regarding the consideration of the bill (see "Opportunities to Waive Parliamentary Rules").

[18] During consideration of appropriations measures, the Committee of the Whole often agrees by unanimous consent to open for amendment at any point a portion of the bill, such as several paragraphs or a title. Such an agreement eliminates the requirement to propose amendments to the specified portion of the bill in sequential order.

[19] The 311(a) point of order enforces total new budget authority and outlays.

[20] U.S. Government Accountability Office, *A Glossary of Terms Used in the Federal Budget Process*, GAO-05-734SP (Washington: GPO, September 2005), p. 91.

[21] *House Manual*, House Rule XXI, clause 2(b) and (c).

[22] Under the FY2009 budget resolution (S.Con.Res. 70, section 301(b), 110th Cong.), budget authority (and the resulting outlays) for FY2008 and FY2009 designated as either for overseas deployment and related activities or as necessary to meet emergency needs are exempt from the 302(f) and 311(a) points of order. While this exemption applies, in part, to appropriations measures and related amendments; in the House, such language is considered legislation on an appropriations bill. Under House precedents, the language creates new law, which would not otherwise exist. Special rules typically waive this rule for provisions in appropriations bills, but typically not amendments.

[23] *Rescissions* cancel previously enacted budget authority. While the House Appropriations Committee may report rescissions, amendments may not add them or increase rescissions in the reported bill.

[24] *House Manual*, House Rule XXI, clause 2(a).

[25] *House Practice*, chapter 4, section 12; p. 84.

[26] Unauthorized appropriations for works and projects in progress are allowed.

[27] In the House, continuing resolutions are not considered general appropriations bills and, therefore, may include unauthorized appropriations. For background information, see CRS Report 97-684, *The Congressional Appropriations Process: An Introduction*, by Sandy Streeter.

[28] Prior to consideration of a regular or supplemental appropriations bill, the House typically adopts a special rule waiving, in part, this rule for the entire bill or the entire bill with selected exceptions.

[29] For more information, see *House Practice*, chapter 4, section 69.

[30] For more information on a "demand for a division of the question," see "Must Be Drafted to Avoid a 'Demand for a Division of the Question'" under reach back amendments below; and *House Manual*, House Rule XVI, clause 5.

[31] In cases in which the amount has already been amended, reachback amendments do not violate House rules prohibiting amendments that would amend text previously amended; since reachback amendments change amounts by reference, as opposed to changing the text.

[32] Representative Garrett, remarks in the House, *Congressional Record* (daily edition), vol. 153, July 19, 2007, p. H8 13 1.

[33] For information on these points of order, see "Spending Ceilings and Offset Amendments" above.

[34] For more information Senate and conference procedures, see CRS Report 97-684, *The Congressional Appropriations Process: An Introduction*, by Sandy Streeter; and CRS Report 97-865, *Points of Order in the Congressional Budget Process*, by James V. Saturno.

[35] See "Must Offset Both Budget Authority and Outlays" under clause 2(f) offset amendments above.

[36] *House Manual*, House Rule XVI, clause 7.

[37] See "May Not Contain Legislation" under clause 2(f) offset amendments above.

[38] *House Manual*, House Rule XXI, clause 2(a).

[39] *House Manual*, section 1058. For an explanation of unauthorized appropriations, see "May Contain Certain Unauthorized Appropriations" under clause 2(f) offset amendments above.

[40] *House Manual*, House Rule XVI, clause 5.

[41] See CRS Report RS2271 1, *Considering Regular Appropriations Bills on the House Floor: Current Practice Regarding Comprehensive Unanimous Consent Agreements*, by Christopher M. Davis.

In: Overview of Congressional Appropriations   ISBN: 978-1-61209-849-4
Editors: J.M. Stewart, D.M. Allworth   © 2011 Nova Science Publishers, Inc.

Chapter 6

LEGISLATIVE BRANCH APPROPRIATIONS BILL: STRUCTURE, CONTENT, AND PROCESS

Lorraine H. Tong

The legislative branch appropriations bill is one of the regular appropriations bills that Congress considers each year. It provides budget authority to spend specified amounts of money for expenditures of the legislative branch for the fiscal year, including staff salaries. This bill funds the operations not only of Congress itself but also of its support agencies and other entities within the legislative branch. Salaries for Members of Congress are not included in the annual bill, but are funded automatically each year in a permanent appropriations account. A detailed examination of legislative branch funding is discussed in CRS Report RL34490, *Legislative Branch: FY2009 Appropriations*, by Ida A. Brudnick. For more information on congressional processes, see *http://www.crs.gov/products/guides/guidehome. shtml.*

CONGRESSIONAL OPERATIONS AND RELATED AGENCIES

Effective in FY2003, Congress restructured the legislative branch appropriations bill so that Title I contains entities that include the House of Representatives, Senate, Joint Items, Capitol Police, Congressional Budget Office, Library of Congress (including the Congressional Research Service),

Architect of the Capitol, Government Accountability Office (formerly named the General Accounting Office), Government Printing Office, Office of Compliance, Open World Leadership Program, and John C. Stennis Center for Public Service. Typically, Title II contains general provisions. Occasionally, the legislative branch bill might contain additional titles for special provisions. Previously, from the late 1970s until FY2003, the bill was divided into two titles: one covered entities that directly supported Congress (Title I: Congressional Operations), and the other covered those that did not exclusively, or almost exclusively, support Congress (Title II: Related Agencies).

Prior to the enactment of the FY2009 Omnibus Appropriations Act (P.L. 111-8) on March 11, 2009, the legislative branch had been funded at the FY2008 budget level under a continuing resolution that covered nine regular appropriations.[1] The FY2009 enacted amount was $4.40 billion, or an approximate 11% increase over the FY2008 enacted amount of $3.97 billion. The House and Senate accounts include budget authority for salaries and other expenses for Member offices, leadership offices, officers and their employees, and committees. Although the legislative branch appropriations bill funds committees annually on a fiscal year basis, each chamber authorizes its committees (except House Appropriations, Senate Appropriations, and Senate Ethics) for two years at a time through resolutions adopted near the beginning of each Congress. The Joint Items account funds the expenses and salaries of the joint committees, the Office of the Attending Physician, the Capitol Guide and Special Services Office, and the preparation of statements of appropriations. Since FY2003, the Capitol Police has been funded under its own separate account, "Capitol Police."

On occasion, supplemental appropriations have been provided to accommodate specific purposes, activities, or unanticipated expenditures.

APPROPRIATION PROCESS

The President proposes spending levels for most annual general appropriations bills that fund activities of executive branch agencies in the President's annual budget, which is submitted by the first Monday in February (31 U.S.C. 1105(a)).[2] However, the House and Senate, including the leadership and the Appropriations Committees, and legislative support agencies develop estimates for the legislative branch entities. The President subsequently presents, without changes in the budget request, the proposed funding levels for the legislative branch submission (31 U.S.C. 1105). The House and Senate Subcommittees on the Legislative Branch each hold hearings at which the heads of legislative entities and the respective chamber's administrative officers explain their requests and answer questions.

The House Appropriations Committee, which traditionally originates appropriations bills, reports a legislative branch appropriations bill that includes funding for the House only, Joint Items, and other legislative branch entities. The House leaves the Senate to determine funding levels for its own operations in the bill.

The Senate Appropriations Committee recommends alterations in funding levels for Joint Items and other legislative branch entities, but customarily makes no revisions in House items. Any differences between House and Senate versions may be reconciled between the two chambers. The President almost always signs the legislative branch bill as passed by the House and Senate.

PERMANENT BUDGET AUTHORITY; TRUST FUNDS

Legislative branch permanent appropriations and trust funds are not included in the legislative branch appropriations act. Permanent appropriations are made available in the amounts necessary for the purposes specified as the result of previously enacted legislation, and do not require annual action. These permanent appropriations include compensation of Members, congressional use of foreign currencies, and Library of Congress payments to copyright owners.

Trust funds are monies held in accounts credited with collections from sources specified by law for defined purposes. Trust funds include gifts and donations to the Library of Congress and funds held by the U.S. Capitol Preservation Commission.

Table 1 presents the various accounts for the FY2008 and FY2009 enacted amounts.

Table 1. Legislative Branch Appropriations, FY2008 and FY2009 (in thousands of dollars)

Entity	FY2008 Enacted	FY2009 Enacted
Senate	831,696	895,030
House of Representatives	1,182,835	1,301,267
Joint Items	23,001	29,220
Capitol Police	281,872	305,750
Office of Compliance	3,342	4,072
Congressional Budget Office	37,306	44,082
Architect of the Capitol	413,471	529,586
Library of Congress, including Congressional Research Service	563,049	607,096
Congressional Research Service, Library of Congress	(102,344)	(107,323)
Government Printing Office	124,688	140,567 a
Government Accountability Office	499,748	531,000
Open World Leadership Program	8,978	13,900
Stennis Center for Public Service	429	430
Title II: General Provisions	0	0
Total Legislative Branch, Titles I and II	**3,970,415**	**4,402,000**

Source: FY2008 funds are contained in P.L. 110-161. FY2009 funds are contained in Division G of the FY2009 Omnibus Appropriations Act , P.L. 111-8.

a. The American Recovery and Reinvestment Act of 2009 (P.L. 111-5) provided an additional $25 million to the Government Accountability Office.

End Notes

[1] On September 30, 2008, the President signed the Consolidated Security, Disaster Assistance, and Continuing Appropriations Act, 2009 (P.L. 110-329, 122 Stat. 3574). Division A, the FY2009 Continuing Appropriations Resolution, extended funding for nine FY2009 regular appropriations bills, including the legislative branch, from October 1, 2008, through March 6, 2009. Subsequently, P.L. 111-6 amended P.L. 110-329 to extend funding through March 11, 2009.

[2] The deadline for the president's budget submission has changed several times over the years. During presidential transition years, there may be delays in its submission. For more details,

see CRS Report RS20752, *Submission of the President's Budget in Transition Years*, by Robert Keith.

In: Overview of Congressional Appropriations   ISBN: 978-1-61209-849-4
Editors: J.M. Stewart, D.M. Allworth   © 2011 Nova Science Publishers, Inc.

Chapter 7

EXAMPLES OF LEGISLATIVE PROVISIONS IN ANNUAL APPROPRIATIONS ACT

Robert Keith

SUMMARY

Over the years, House and Senate rules generally have been used to promote the separate consideration of substantive legislation and measures providing annual appropriations to federal agencies, chiefly so that the regular funding of the federal government is not impeded by controversies associated with authorizing and other legislation.

The key rules upon which this separation is based are House Rule XXI and Senate Rule XVI. On July 26, 1999, the Senate agreed to S.Res. 160, a measure effectively overturning a 1995 precedent that had caused the Senate's ban against considering legislative provisions in annual appropriations acts not to be enforced for several years.

The procedural separation, however, is not ironclad because (1) the rules are not self-enforcing; (2) the rules may be waived in various ways; and (3) the rules are not fully comprehensive in their coverage and application.

Legislative provisions may generate controversy with any type of annual appropriations act, including regular, continuing, and supplemental appropriations acts. The most visible controversies in recent years often have been associated with omnibus appropriations acts, which are measures that combine two or more regular appropriations acts. During the 1980s and 1990s and continuing into the 2000s, there has been a greater use of omnibus appropriations acts; in some instances, a considerable portion of these omnibus appropriations acts has consisted of legislative provisions.

This report illustrates House and Senate practices regarding legislative provisions by listing dozens of major legislative provisions that were included in 13 omnibus appropriations acts enacted in recent years, as well legislative provisions included in recent supplemental appropriations acts. In addition, the report lists more than a dozen legislative provisions that were dropped from three of the omnibus appropriations acts.

The report will be updated as developments warrant. (For more information on omnibus appropriations acts, see CRS Report RL3 2473, *Omnibus Appropriations Acts: Overview of Recent Practices*, by Robert Keith.)

THE SEPARATION OF LEGISLATION AND APPROPRIATIONS

For well over a century, the House and Senate have had rules meant to promote the separate consideration of substantive legislation and measures providing annual appropriations to federal agencies. The chief reason behind this procedural division is to ensure that the regular funding of the federal government is not impeded by controversies associated with authorizing and other legislation that establishes and organizes agencies, authorizes and reauthorizes programs, and sets forth policy guidelines and restrictions.

Despite these rules, substantive legislation sometimes is included in annual appropriations acts. Provisions in annual appropriations acts carrying substantive legislation are referred to as "legislative provisions."[1]

The House and Senate Appropriations Committees typically report three different types of annual appropriations acts each year. Each of the House and Senate Appropriations subcommittees develop one regular appropriations act, which provides budget authority to federal agencies for the upcoming fiscal year.[2] Supplemental appropriations acts provide additional budget authority during the fiscal year when the regular appropriation is insufficient, or to finance activities not provided for in the regular appropriation. Continuing appropriations acts, also called continuing resolutions, provide stop-gap funding for agencies that have not yet received a regular appropriation.

An *omnibus* appropriations act generally is regarded as a regular appropriations act or a continuing resolution that has been expanded to encompass agencies and accounts normally covered in two or more of the regular appropriations acts. In the case of a continuing resolution that is an omnibus appropriations act, it typically goes beyond formula-funding for multiple bills to include the full text of the regular appropriations acts.

House Rule XXI

In the House, Rule XXI is intended to keep the consideration of annual appropriations acts separate from the consideration of substantive legislation. Clauses 2(b) and 2(c) of the rule prohibit the inclusion of "legislative provisions" (i.e, provisions changing existing law or otherwise carrying substantive law) in *general* appropriations bills reported by the committee or offered as floor amendments. In addition, Clause 4 prohibits the inclusion of appropriations in legislation reported by any committee other than the Appropriations Committee.[3] The House, unlike the Senate, does not regard continuing resolutions to be general appropriations bills.

Senate Rule XVI

In the Senate, Rule XVI serves to separate the consideration of legislative and appropriations matters in a fashion similar to that employed by the House. In 1995, however, during the Senate's consideration of a supplemental appropriations bill, the chair's ruling that a particular amendment offered by a Senator was out of order as legislation was overturned by the full Senate; this action came to be referred to as the "Hutchison precedent."[4] In the aftermath of that ruling, the Senate for several years did not enforce the portion of the rule prohibiting legislative provisions in annual appropriations acts. On July 26, 1999, the Senate agreed by a vote of 53 to 45 to S.Res. 160, a measure effectively overturning the Hutchison precedent and restoring the long-standing prohibition against legislative provisions.[5]

In addition, Senate Rule XXVIII in part bars conferees from inserting new matter (i.e., matter not in the bills passed by either body) into a conference report. In 1996, in an action known as the "FedEx precedent," the Senate overturned a ruling of the chair, thereby allowing new matter to be included in a conference report. As a consequence of this action, the restriction in Rule XXVIII against the inclusion of new matter in conference reports was not enforced for several years. In the case of annual appropriations acts, the suspension of this part of Rule XXVIII facilitated the inclusion of legislative provisions during this period. Toward the end of the 106th Congress, a provision overturning the FedEx precedent (effective at the beginning of the 107th Congress) was enacted as part of the Consolidated Omnibus Appropriations Act for FY200 1.[6]

INCLUSION OF LEGISLATIVE PROVISIONS IN APPROPRIATIONS ACTS

Although House and Senate rules and practices over the decades have promoted the separate consideration of legislation and appropriations, the separation has not been ironclad. In many instances, during the routine operation of the annual appropriations process, minor provisions are included in appropriations acts that technically may be regarded under the rules as legislative in nature, but do not significantly undermine the dichotomy between legislation and appropriations. At other times, however, the legislative provisions included in annual appropriations acts have been much more substantial and have represented a deliberate suspension of the usual procedural boundaries.

In the House and Senate, legislative provisions may be included in annual appropriations acts in several ways, as discussed below.

Rules Are Not Self-Enforcing

First, the rules that enforce the boundaries between legislation and appropriations are not self- enforcing. For a potential violation to be stopped, a Member must successfully raise a point of order and it must be sustained if challenged.

Rules May Be Waived

Second, like any other rules of the House and Senate, these rules may be waived in various ways. In the House, for example, it is not uncommon to waive Rule XXI under a "special rule," reported by the House Rules

Committee, governing consideration of the annual appropriations act. The Senate sometimes effectively waives its rules when it considers legislation under unanimous consent agreements.

Rules Are Not Comprehensive

Finally, the rules are not fully comprehensive in their coverage and application. Both House Rule XXI and Senate Rule XVI afford some exceptions, particularly in the Senate. For example, the House, as previously mentioned, does not regard continuing resolutions to be general appropriations bills; consequently, the prohibitions under Rule XXI do not apply to their consideration. Further, while the Senate's restrictions against legislative provisions apply to amendments of the Senate Appropriations Committee made to a House-passed appropriations act, they do not apply to legislative provisions originated by the committee in a Senate-numbered appropriations act. In recent years, the Senate Appropriations Committee has originated a greater number of annual appropriations acts (i.e., acting on a Senate-numbered measure, rather than a House-passed measure, up to the stage of final action), thereby circumventing the Rule XVI prohibitions against legislative provisions.

It should be noted that a provision in an appropriations act generally is determined to be legislative by a ruling of the chair. In the Senate, the Members sometimes decide the matter by a vote, upon the raising of a point of order or an appeal of the chair's ruling. The provisions listed in this report, therefore, should be regarded only as "possibly" legislative in nature; although they meet criteria long used by the House and Senate to determine whether a provision is legislative, no ruling was made by the chair or the Senate in these cases. Many of the examples provided in the report explicitly state that they amend an existing law and cite a public law number or a section of the *United States Code* (often, a marginal note is provided in the slip law indicating the applicable section of the U.S.C.).

RECENT PRACTICES

The inclusion of legislative provisions in annual appropriations acts has been a long-standing feature of the appropriations process. In many instances, legislative provisions are regarded as routine or technical and do not generate controversy. In other cases, legislative provisions may spark contentious debate, complicating and prolonging the consideration of the underlying appropriations measure.

Controversies regarding the use of legislative provisions sometimes arise in connection with the consideration of regular, continuing, and supplemental appropriations acts, particularly when such acts have been chosen by the House and Senate leadership as vehicles to carry other legislative matters. Controversies probably occur less often in the case of continuing resolutions, because these stop-gap funding measures usually are considered under circumstances where the pressures are greater to keep the measures "clean" and free of provisions that would impede their timely enactment.

With respect to regular and supplemental appropriations acts, the latter type of annual appropriations act is more likely to have been used in recent years as a vehicle for significant legislative matters. A recent supplemental appropriations act, for example, included separate titles dealing with funding shortfalls in a mandatory health program, an increase in the minimum wage, small business tax incentives, and other matters typically addressed outside of the annual appropriations process.

Examples of legislative provisions included in recent supplemental appropriations acts are shown (in reverse chronological order) in **Table 1**. For each legislative provision, the subject matter is identified—if the provision is given a short title, such as the "Post-9/11 Veterans Educational Assistance Act of 2008," it is listed—and the *Statutes-at-Large* citation is provided. The listing of legislative provisions in **Table 1** (and in the other tables) for each act is intended merely to be illustrative; it does not represent a comprehensive or systematic survey and should not be used to assess or infer any trends in House and Senate practices.

Although legislative provisions may generate controversy with any type of annual appropriations act, the most visible controversies in recent years have tended to be associated with "omnibus," "consolidated," or "omnibus consolidated" appropriations acts, which merge two or more of the regular appropriations acts into a single measure.[7]

Table 1. Examples of Legislative Provisions Included in Supplemental Appropriations Acts

Supplemental Appropriations Act/ Legislative Provisiona	Statutes-at-Large Citation
1. Supplemental Appropriations Act, 2009 (P.L. 111-32; June 24, 2009)	
Marine Gunnery Sergeant John David Fry Scholarship	123 Stat. 1889-1890
International Development Association	123 Stat. 1901-1902
Promotion of Policy Goals at the World Bank Group	123 Stat. 1902-1903
Climate Change Mitigation and Greenhouse Gas Accounting	123 Stat. 1903-1904
Consumer Assistance to Recycle and Save Program ("Cash for Clunkers")	123 Stat. 1909-1915
2. Supplemental Appropriations Act, 2008 (P.L. 110-252; June 30, 2008)	
Combat Veterans Debt Elimination Act of 2008	122 Stat. 2327-2328
Emergency Unemployment Compensation	122 Stat. 2353-2357
Post-9/11 Veterans Educational Assistance Act of 2008	122 Stat. 2357-2386
Close the Contractor Fraud Loophole Act of 2008	122 Stat. 2386-2387
Government Funding Transparency Act of 2008	122 Stat. 2387
Medicaid Provisions	122 Stat. 2387-2396
3. U.S. Troop Readiness, Veterans' Care, Katrina Recovery, and Iraq Accountability Appropriations Act, 2007 (P.L. 110-28; May 28, 2007)	
Award of Medal of Honor to Woodrow W. Keeble for Valor During Korean Was	121 Stat. 138
Elimination of SCHIP Shortfall and Other Health Matters	121 Stat. 186-188
Fair Minimum Wage Act of 2007	121 Stat. 188-189
Small Business and Work Opportunity Tax Act of 2007	121 Stat. 190-204
Small Business and Work Opportunity Act of 2007	121 Stat. 204-211
4. Military Construction Appropriations and Emergency Hurricane Supplemental Appropriations Act, 2005 (P.L. 108-324; October13, 2004)	
Alaska Natural Gas Pipeline Act	118 Stat. 1255-1267
5. Emergency Wartime Supplemental Appropriations Act, 2003 (P.L. 108-11; April 16, 2003)	
Columbia Orbiter Memorial Act	117 Stat. 603-604

Table 1. (Continued)

Supplemental Appropriations Act/ Legislative Provisiona	Statutes-at-Large Citation
Additional Temporary Extended Unemployment Compensation for Displaced Airline Related Workers	117 Stat. 607-609
Panel to Review Sexual Misconduct Allegations at United States Air Force Academy	117 Stat. 609-610

Source: Prepared by the Congressional Research Service (using the cited public laws in slip law form).

a. A provision in an appropriations act is determined to be "legislative" by a ruling of the chair or a vote of the chamber, upon the raising of a point of order or appeal. The provisions listed in this table, therefore, should be regarded only as "possibly legislative" in nature; although they meet criteria long used by the House and Senate to determine whether a provision is legislative, no ruling was made by the chair or the chamber in these cases. The listing is intended merely to be illustrative; it does not represent a comprehensive or systematic survey and should not be used to assess or infer any trends in House and Senate practices.

Table 2. Omnibus Appropriations Acts: FY1 986-FY2009

Act	Public Law Number	Date of Enactment
1. Further Continuing Appropriations Act, 1986	P.L. 99-190	December 19, 1985
2. Continuing Appropriations Act, 1987	P.L. 99-500	October 18, 1986
3. Further Continuing Appropriations Act, 1988	P.L. 100-202	December 22, 1987
4. Omnibus Consolidated Rescissions and Appropriations Act of 1996	P.L. 104-134	April 26, 1996
5. Omnibus Consolidated Appropriations Act, 1997	P.L. 104-208	September 30, 1996
6. Omnibus Consolidated and Emergency Supplemental Appropriations Act, 1999	P.L. 105-277	October 21, 1998
7. Consolidated Appropriations Act, 2000	P.L. 106-113	November 29, 1999

Table 2. (Continued)

Act	Public Law Number	Date of Enactment
8. Consolidated Appropriations Act, 2001	P.L. 106-554	December 21, 2000
9. VA-HUD Appropriations Act, 2001	P.L. 106-377	October 27, 2000
10. Consolidated Appropriations Resolu-tion, 2003	P.L. 108-7	February 20, 2003
11. Consolidated Appropriations Act, 2004	P.L. 108-199	January 23, 2004
12. Consolidated Appropriations Act, 2005	P.L. 108-447	December 8, 2004
13. Revised Continuing Appropriations Resolution, 2007	P.L. 110-5	February 15, 2007
14. Consolidated Appropriations Act, 2008	P.L. 110-161	December 26, 2007
15. Consolidated Security, Disaster Assist-ance, and Continuing Appropriations Act, 2009	P.L. 110-329	September 30, 2008
16. Omnibus Appropriations Act, 2009	P.L. 111-8	March 11, 2009

Source: Prepared by the Congressional Research Service.

Beginning in the 1980s, various factors have contributed to the greater use of omnibus appropriations acts, particularly escalating disagreements between the President and Congress over general budgetary policy and policies in key program areas, and the resultant legislative gridlock. At first, the omnibus appropriations acts took the form of continuing resolutions, but in recent years they mostly have taken the form of bills.

Table 2 lists the 16 most recent omnibus appropriations acts.

Table 3 provides examples (in reverse chronological order) of legislative provisions that were included in those omnibus appropriations acts.

In some instances, a considerable portion of these omnibus appropriations acts has consisted of legislative provisions. Two reasons for this practice are that : (1) legislation stalled at the end of a session, that otherwise might not advance, can be carried through to enactment on the funding bill, which is considered to be "must-pass" legislation; and (2) popular legislative provisions may be added to an appropriations act to increase its chances of enactment.

The practice of including major legislative provisions in annual appropriations acts, particularly omnibus acts, generates controversy for several reasons. Some Members decry the practice as undermining the deliberative process. They assert that in many instances the inclusion of such provisions in lengthy and complex appropriations bills considered toward the close of a session may require Members to vote on matters with which they are largely unfamiliar, may give them too little time to debate these matters, may usurp the prerogatives of the relevant authorizing committees, and may shield from proper scrutiny legislation that would not prevail on its own merits.

Advocates of the practice, however, argue that it provides needed flexibility to the legislative process, allowing Congress to process and complete its business more efficiently, especially in the waning days of a session. Many such provisions, they maintain, already have been given a thorough review under regular procedures. Further, their inclusion in annual appropriations bills often is at the behest of authorizing committee members, who have not been able to advance their legislation because of a crowded legislative agenda.

In 2004, circumstances in the Senate prompted some to advance another argument in favor of using an omnibus appropriations act for FY2005. By the beginning of the appropriations cycle for FY2005, the Senate had not agreed to the conference report on the FY2005 budget resolution (S.Con.Res. 95). Consequently, one of the principal procedural tools used to encourage spending restraint—points of order to enforce spending allocations to the Appropriations subcommittees under Section 302(b) of the Congressional Budget Act of 1 974—was not available. The Senate, however, had imposed a ceiling of $814 billion on total appropriations for FY2005 (enforceable by a point of order) in the prior year's budget resolution, which still was in effect. In order for the ceiling on total FY2005 appropriations to be enforced at that time, however, all of the regular appropriations bills for that fiscal year would have had to been considered in a single, omnibus measure. (Although the House and Senate did not reach final agreement on the FY2005 budget resolution, the Senate adopted a "deeming resolution" later in the session that resolved the enforcement problem for the remainder of the budget cycle.)[8]

The Consolidated Appropriations Act for FY2000 (P.L. 106-113) and the Consolidated Appropriations Act for FY2001 (P.L. 106-554) enacted several appropriations bills and legislative bills by cross-reference.

Although the House and Senate regularly incorporate major legislative provisions into annual appropriations acts, Members often are successful in getting legislative provisions dropped from such acts. **Table 4** provides a listing of legislative provisions dropped from three of the omnibus appropriations acts listed in the previous table. As with the other tables, the listing is intended merely to be illustrative.

For the sake of expedience, the examples provided in **Table 4** were drawn from articles contained in the *CQ Almanac* (for calendar year 1996) and the *CQ Monitor* (for calendar year 1998). In the case of the three omnibus appropriations acts listed in the table, all of the legislative provisions were dropped in conference; however, such provisions sometimes are dropped at earlier stages of the legislative process. Whether the provision originated in the House or the Senate is indicated. In this context, origination in a chamber means that it was offered in the markup of the Appropriations Committee or subcommittee of that chamber, was offered during floor consideration by that chamber, or was proposed in conference by the conferees of that chamber.

The three omnibus appropriations acts incorporated the full text of several of the regular appropriations acts. Legislative provisions listed under these omnibus acts may have been dropped in the conference on the omnibus act, or beforehand in a conference on one of the regular appropriations acts subsequently incorporated into the omnibus act.

On many occasions, the House and Senate resolved controversy over a contentious legislative provision by adopting a substantial modification of it rather than dropping it altogether. This report does not address such practices.

Table 3. Examples of Legislative Provisions Included in Omnibus Appropriations Acts

Omnibus Appropriations Act / Legislative Provision	Statutes-at-Large Citation
1. Omnibus Appropriations Act, 2009 (P.L. 111-8; March 11, 2009)	
Afghan Allies Protection Act of 2009	123 Stat. 807-811
Integrated University Program	123 Stat. 627-628
Christopher Columbus Fellowship Authorization	123 Stat. 678
Nonreduction in Pay While Federal Employee is Performing Active Service in the Uniformed Services or National Guard	123 Stat. 693-695
Pay Freeze for Members of Congress in 2010	123 Stat. 988
2. Consolidated Security, Disaster Assistance, and Continuing Appropriations Act,	
Allocation and Use of Campus-Based Higher Education	122 Stat. 3596-3597

Assistance	
Wartime Suspension of Statute of Limitations Applicable to Certain Offenses	122 Stat. 3647

Table 3. (Continued)

Omnibus Appropriations Act / Legislative Provision	Statutes-at-Large Citation
Incentives for Additional Downblending of Highly Enriched Uranium by the Russian Federation	122 Stat. 3647-3651
Recurrent Training of Aliens in Operation of Aircraft	122 Stat. 3689
3. Consolidated Appropriations Act, 2008 (P.L. 110-161; December 26, 2007)a	
Extension of Agricultural Programs	121 Stat. 1883-1884
Emergency Steel Loan Guarantee Act of 1999 Amendments	121 Stat. 1892-1893
Harmful Algal Bloom and Hypoxia Research and Control Act of 1998 Amendments	121 Stat. 1930
ED 1.0 Act	121 Stat. 1932-1934
Inland Empire and Cucamonga Valley Recycling Projects	121 Stat. 1954-1955
Redesign and Issuance of Circulating Quarter Dollar Honoring the District of Columbia and Each of the Territories	121 Stat. 2016-2018
Requirement for Public-Private Competition	121 Stat. 2029-2031
Amendments Relating to the Civil Service Retirement System, Amendments Relating to the Federal Employees' Retirement System, and Related Provisions	121 Stat. 2075-2078
Extension of the Implementation Deadline for the Western Hemisphere Travel Initiative	121 Stat. 2080
Secure Handling of Ammonium Nitrate	121 Stat. 2083-2090
Kids in Disasters Well-being, Safety, and Health Act of 2007	121 Stat. 2213-2217
Relief for Iraqi, Montagnards, Hmong and Other Refugees Who Do Not Pose a Threat to the United States	121 Stat. 2364-2366
4. Revised Continuing Appropriations Resolution, 2007 (P.L. 110-5; February 25, 2007)	
Inter-American Development Bank Act Amendment	121 Stat. 25
Workforce Investment Act of 1998 Amendment	121 Stat. 30-31
5. Consolidated Appropriations Act, 2005 (P.L. 108-447; December 8, 2004)	
Patent and Trademark Fees	118 Stat. 2924-2930
Oceans and Human Health Act	118 Stat. 2930-2934
Reform of the Board of Directors of the Tennessee Valley Authority	118 Stat. 2963-2967
Gaylord A. Nelson Apostle Islands National Lakeshore Wilderness Act	118 Stat. 3069-3070

Migratory Bird Treaty Reform Act of 2004	118 Stat. 3071-3072
Age Requirement for Senate Pages	118 Stat. 3170
Terrorism and Financial Intelligence	118 Stat. 3242-3246

Table 3. (Continued)

Omnibus Appropriations Act / Legislative Provision	Statutes-at-Large Citation
Denali Commission Act of 1998 Amendment	118 Stat. 3268
Housing and Community Development Act of 1987 Amendment	118 Stat. 3319-3320
Designation of National Tree	118 Stat. 3344
Designation of National Veterans Memorial (Mt. Soledad)	118 Stat. 3346-3347
225th Anniversary of the American Revolution Commemoration Act	118 Stat. 3348-3350
Rural Air Service Improvements Act of 2004	118 Stat. 3350-3351
L-1 Visa and H-1B Visa Reform Act	118 Stat. 3352-3361
National Aviation Heritage Area Act	118 Stat. 3361-3368
Mississippi Gulf Coast National Heritage Area Act	118 Stat. 3374-3377
Satellite Home Viewer Extension and Reauthorization Act of 2004	118 Stat. 3393-3431
Snake River Water Rights Act of 2004	118 Stat. 3341-3441
Small Business Reauthorization and Manufacturing Assistance Act of 2004	118 Stat. 3441-3466
6. Consolidated Appropriations Act, 2004 (P.L. 108-199; January 23, 2004)	
Sun Grant Research Initiative Act of 2003	118 Stat. 41-44
HELP Commission Act	118 Stat. 101-106
Alaskan Fisheries	118 Stat. 108-110
DC School Choice Incentive Act of 2003	118 Stat. 126-134
Denial of Visas to Supporters of Colombian Illegal Armed Groups	118 Stat. 194
Administrative Provisions Related to Multilateral Development Institutions	118 Stat. 202-204
Millennium Challenge Act of 2003	118 Stat. 211-226
Designation of Senator Paul D. Wellstone NIH MDCRC Program	118 Stat. 255
Special Study of Simplification of Need Analysis and Application for Title IV Aid	118 Stat. 263-266
Motorist Information Concerning Pharmacy Services	118 Stat. 296-297
Study on Earned Income Tax Credit Certification Program	118 Stat. 319-320
Oklahoma City National Memorial Act Amendments of 2003	118 Stat. 347-349
Amendment to the McKinney-Vento Homeless	118 Stat. 394

Assistance Act	
Designations of Areas for PM2.5 and Submission of Implementation Plans for Regional Haze	118 Stat. 417

Table 3. (Continued)

Omnibus Appropriations Act / Legislative Provision	Statutes-at-Large Citation
Treatment of Pioneer Homes in Alaska as State Home for Veterans	118 Stat. 417-418
Pesticide Registration Improvement Act of 2003	118 Stat. 419-434
Commission on the Abraham Lincoln Study Abroad Fellowship Program	118 Stat. 435-437
Congaree National Park Boundary Revision	118 Stat. 442
Theodore Roosevelt National Wildlife Refuge	118 Stat. 443-444
The Unites States Senate-China Interparliamentary Group	118 Stat. 448-449
Recomputation of Benefits Guaranteed in Connection With the Termination of the Republic Steel Retirement Plan	118 Stat. 450-451
7. Consolidated Appropriations Resolution, 2003 (P.L. 108-7; February 20, 2003)	
District of Columbia Charter School Fund	117 Stat. 132-133
Moccasin Bend Archeological District Act	117 Stat. 247-249
T'uf Shur Bien Preservation Trust Area Act	117 Stat. 279-294
National Forest Organizational Camp Fee Improvement Act of 2003	117 Stat. 294-297
Transfer of the Library of Congress Police to the United States Capitol Police	117 Stat. 362-364
Inclusion of Towers in Airport Development	117 Stat. 424-427
Endowment for Presidential Libraries	117 Stat. 462
NASA Enhanced-Use Lease of Real Property Demonstration	117 Stat. 525-526
Homeland Security Act of 2002	117 Stat. 526-532
Amendments Agricultural Assistance Act of 2003	117 Stat. 538-547
TANF and Medicare	117 Stat. 548
Price-Anderson Act Amendments	117 Stat. 551
United States-China Economic and Security Review Commission	117 Stat. 552-553
8. VA-HUD Appropriations Act for FY2001 (P.L. 106-377; October 27, 2000)	
Technical Amendments and Corrections to the National Housing Act	114 Stat. 1441A-25
Computer Access for Public Housing Residents	114 Stat. 1441A-27
Native American Eligibility for the Ross Program	114 Stat. 1441A-29 114
Filipino Veterans' Benefits Improvements	Stat. 1441A-57 through 58
Amendment to Irrigation Project Contract Extension Act	114 Stat. 1441A-70

| of 1998 | |
| Scope of Authority of Secretary of Energy to Modify Organization of National Nuclear Security Administration | 114 Stat. 1441A-81 |

Table 3. (Continued)

Omnibus Appropriations Act / Legislative Provision	Statutes-at-Large Citation
9. Consolidated Appropriations Act, 2001 (P.L. 106-554; December 21, 2000)	
Basic Charter School Grant Program (H.R. 5656 enacted by cross-reference)	114 Stat. 2763A57 through 62
Assets for Independence Act Amendments of 2000 (H.R. 5656 enacted by cross-reference)	114 Stat. 2763A74 through 76
Physical Education for Progress Act (H.R. 5656 enacted by cross-reference)	114 Stat. 2763A76 through 79
Early Learning Opportunities Acts (H.R. 5656 enacted by cross-reference)	114 Stat. 2763A79 through 89
Rural Education Achievement Program (H.R. 5656 enacted by cross-reference)	114 Stat. 2763A89 through 92
Mandatory Removal From Employment of Federal Law Enforcement Officers Convicted of Felonies (H.R. 5658 enacted by cross-reference)	114 Stat. 2763A167 through 169
Wet Weather Watershed Pilot Projects (H.R. 5666 enacted by cross-reference)	114 Stat. 2763A225
Vietnam Education Foundation Act of 2000 (H.R. 5666 enacted by cross-reference)	114 Stat. 2763A254 through 258
Colorado Ute Settlement Act Amendments of 2000 (H.R. 5666 enacted by cross-reference)	114 Stat. 2763A258 through 266
Designation of American Museum of Science and Energy (H.R. 5666 enacted by cross-reference)	114 Stat. 2763A266 through 268
Delta Regional Authority Act of 2000 (H.R. 5666 enacted by cross-reference)	114 Stat. 2763A268 through 281
Dakota Water Resources Act of 2000 (H.R. 5666 enacted by cross-reference)	114 Stat. 2763A281 through 293
Sioux Nation Supreme Court and National Native American Mediation Training Center (H.R. 5666 enacted by cross-reference)	114 Stat. 2763A293 through 295
Erie Canalway National Heritage Corridor Act (H.R. 5666 enacted by cross-reference)	114 Stat. 2763A295 through 303
Law Enforcement Pay Equity Act of 2000 (H.R. 5666 enacted by cross-reference)	114 Stat. 2763A303 through 310
Honoring the Navajo Code Talkers (H.R. 5666 enacted by cross-reference)	114 Stat. 2763A311 through 312
Certain Alaskan Cruise Ship Operations (H.R. 5666 enacted by cross-reference)	114 Stat. 2763A315 through 323
LIFE [Legal Immigration Family Equity] Act	114 Stat. 2763A324

Amendments of 2000 (H.R. 5666 enacted by cross-reference)	through 328

Table 3. (Continued)

Omnibus Appropriations Act / Legislative Provision	Statutes-at-Large Citation
Literacy Involves Families Together Act (H.R. 5666 enacted by cross-reference)	114 Stat. 2763A328 through 335
Children's Internet Protection Act (H.R. 5666 enacted by cross-reference)	114 Stat. 2763A335 through 352
Black Rock Desert-High Rock Canyon Emigrant Trails National Conservation Area Act of 2000 (H.R. 5666 enacted by cross-reference)	114 Stat. 2763A353 through 357
Jamestown 400th Commemoration Commission Act of 2000 (H.R. 5666 enacted by cross-reference)	114 Stat. 2763A359 through 363
Commodity Futures Modernization Act of 2000 (H.R. 5660 enacted by cross-reference)	114 Stat. 2763A365 through 461
Medicare, Medicaid, and SCHIP Benefits Improvement and Protection Act of 2000 (H.R. 5661 enacted by cross-reference)	114 Stat. 2763A463 through 586
Community Renewal Tax Relief Act of 2000 (H.R. 5662 enacted by cross-reference)	114 Stat. 2763A587 through 651
New Markets Venture Capital Program Act of 2000 (H.R. 5663 enacted by cross-reference)	114 Stat. 2763A653 through 666
Small Business Reauthorization Act of 2000 (H.R. 5667 enacted by cross-reference)	114 Stat. 2763A667 through 710
10. Consolidated Appropriations Act, 2000 (P.L. 106-113; November 29, 1999)	
Silk Road Strategy Act of 1999 (H.R. 3422 enacted by cross-reference)	113 Stat. 1501A123 through 126
Mississippi National Forest Improvement Act of 1999 (H.R. 3423 enacted by cross-reference)	113 Stat. 1501A210 through 214
Early Detection, Diagnosis, and Interventions for Newborns and Infants With Hearing Loss (H.R. 3424 enacted by cross-reference)	113 Stat. 1501A276 through 280
Denali Commission (H.R. 3424 enacted by cross-reference)	113 Stat. 1501A280
Welfare-to-Work and Child Support Amendments of 1999 (H.R. 3424 enacted by cross-reference)	113 Stat. 1501A280 through 287
International Debt Relief (H.R. 3425 enacted by cross-reference)	113 Stat. 1501A311 through 318
Survivor Benefits (H.R. 3425 enacted by cross-reference)	113 Stat. 1501A318
Medicare, Medicaid, and SCHIP Balanced Budget Refinement Act of 1999 (H.R. 3426 enacted by cross-reference)	113 Stat. 1501A321 through 403

| Admiral James W. Nance and Meg Donovan Foreign Relations Authorization Act, Fiscal Years 2000 and 2001 (H.R. 3427 enacted by cross-reference) | 113 Stat. 1501A405 through 520 |

Table 3. (Continued)

Omnibus Appropriations Act / Legislative Provision	Statutes-at-Large Citation
Intellectual Property and Communications Omnibus Reform Act of 1999 (S. 1948 enacted by cross-reference)	113 Stat. 1501A521 through 603
Paygo Adjustments	113 Stat. 1536-1537
11. Omnibus Consolidated and Emergency Supplemental Appropriations Act, 1999 (P.L. 105-277; October 21, 1998)	
Lorton Technical Corrections Act of 1998	112 Stat. 2681-600 through 603
Olympic and Amateur Sports Act Amendments of 1998	112 Stat. 2681-603 through 609
Federal Vacancies Reform Act of 1998	112 Stat. 2681-611 through 616
American Fisheries Act	112 Stat. 2681-616 through 637
Denali Commission Act of 1998	112 Stat. 2681-637 through 641
American Competitiveness and Workforce Improvement Act of 1998	112 Stat. 2681-641 through 658
Salton Sea Feasibility Study	112 Stat. 2681-658 through 660
Cheyenne River Sioux Tribe, Lower Brule Sioux Tribe, and State of South Dakota Terrestrial Wildlife Habitat Restoration	112 Stat. 2681-660 through 670
Office of National Drug Control Policy Reauthorization Act of 1998	112 Stat. 2681-670 through 693
Western Hemisphere Drug Elimination Act	112 Stat. 2681-693 through 707
Drug-Free Workplace Act of 1998	112 Stat. 2681-707 through 710
Canyon Ferry Reservoir, Montana, Act	112 Stat. 2681-710 through 718
Internet Tax Freedom Act	112 Stat. 2681-719 through 726
Other Provisions [regarding Internet taxes]	112 Stat. 2681-726 through 728
Children's Online Privacy Protection Act of 1998	112 Stat. 2681-728 through 735
Vaccine Injury Compensation Program Modification Act	112 Stat. 2681-741 through 742

| Persian Gulf War Veterans Act of 1998 | 112 Stat. 2681-742 through 749 |

Table 3. (Continued)

Omnibus Appropriations Act / Legislative Provision	Statutes-at-Large Citation
Child Online Protection Act	112 Stat. 2681-736 through 741
Government Paperwork Elimination Act	112 Stat. 2681-749 through 751
Drug Demand Reduction Act	112 Stat. 2681-751 through 759
Methamphetamine Trafficking Penalty Enhancement Act of 1998	112 Stat. 2681-759 through 760
Not Legalizing Marijuana for Medicinal Use	112 Stat. 2681-760 through 761
Foreign Affairs Reform and Restructuring Act of 1998	112 Stat. 2681-761 through 854
Depository Institutions-GSE Affiliation Act of 1998	112 Stat. 2681-854 through 856
Chemical Weapons Convention Implementation Act of 1998	112 Stat. 2681-856 through 886
Tax and Trade Relief Extension Act of 1998	112 Stat. 2681-886 through 918
Pay-As-You-Go Provision	112 Stat. 2681-919
12. Omnibus Consolidated Appropriations Act, 1997 (P.L. 104-208; September 30, 1996)	
Age Discrimination in Employment Amendments of 1996	110 Stat. 3009-23 through 25
Child Pornography Prevention Act of 1996	110 Stat. 3009-26 through 31
NATO Enlargement Facilitation Act of 1996	110 Stat. 3009-173 through 178
Student Loan Marketing Association Reorganization Act of 1996	110 Stat. 3009-275 through 293
Museum and Library Services Act of 1996	110 Stat. 3009-293 through 314
Thrift Savings Investment Funds Act of 1996	110 Stat. 3009-372 through 374
Thrift Savings Plan Act of 1996	110 Stat. 3009-374 through 378
Federal Financial Management Improvement Act of 1996	110 Stat. 3009-389 through 394
Economic Growth and Regulatory Paperwork Reduction	110 Stat. 3009-394 through

Act of 1996	499
Adjustment of PAYGO Balances	110 Stat. 3009-500

Table 3. (Continued)

Omnibus Appropriations Act / Legislative Provision	Statutes-at-Large Citation
Amendments to District of Columbia School Reform Act of 1995	110 Stat. 3009-503 through 507
Oregon Resource Conservation Act of 1996	110 Stat. 3009-523 through 545
Illegal Immigration Reform and Immigrant Responsibility Act of 1996	110 Stat. 3009-546 through 724
Small Business Programs Improvement Act of 1996	110 Stat. 3009-724 through 747
California Bay-Delta Environmental Enhancement and Water Security Act	110 Stat. 3009-748 through 749
13. Omnibus Consolidated Rescissions and Appropriations Act of 1996 (P.L. 104-134; April 26, 1996)	
Amendments to the Violent Crime Control and Law Enforcement Act of 1994	110 Stat. 1321-14 through 22
Prison Litigation Reform Act of 1995	110 Stat. 1321-66 through 77
District of Columbia School Reform Act of 1995	110 Stat. 1321-107 through 156
Amendments to the Goals 2000: Educate America Act	110 Stat. 1321-251 through 257
FDA Export Reform and Enhancement Act of 1996	110 Stat. 1321-313 through 320
USEC [U.S. Enrichment Corporation] Privatization Act	110 Stat. 1321-335 through 354
Debt Collection Improvement Act of 1996	110 Stat. 1321-358 through 380
14. Further Continuing Appropriations for Fiscal Year 1988 (P.L. 100-202; December 22, 1987)	
Cancellation of FY1998 Sequester Order Special House and Senate Procedures for Considering Requests for the Nicaraguan Resistance	101 Stat. 1329 101 Stat. 1329-437 through 441
Warren G. Magnuson Foundation and Margaret Chase Smith Foundation Assistance Act Authorization and Grants Agriculture Aid and Trade Missions Act	101 Stat. 1329-442 through 443 101 Stat. 1329-446 through 450
15. Continuing Appropriations for Fiscal Year 1987 (P.L. 99-591; October 30, 1986)	
Defense Acquisition Improvement Act of 1986	100 Stat. 3341-130 through 177

| Paperwork Reduction Reauthorization Act of 1986
Human Rights in Romania | 100 Stat. 3341-335 through
345 100 Stat. 3341-353
through 354 |

Table 3. (Continued)

Omnibus Appropriations Act / Legislative Provision	Statutes-at-Large Citation
School Lunch and Child Nutrition Amendments of 1986 Aviation Safety Commission Act of 1986	100 Stat. 3341-362 through 373 100 Stat. 3341-373 through 376
Metropolitan Washington Airports Act of 1986	100 Stat. 3341-376 through 388
16. Further Continuing Appropriations for Fiscal Year 1986 (P.L. 99-190; December 19, 1985)	
Revisions to Defense Contract Allowable Cost Provision (10 U.S.C. 2324)	99 Stat. 1223-1224
United States Holocaust Memorial Council	99 Stat. 1267
Amendment to Title XI of the Federal Aviation Act of 1958	99 Stat. 1289
Ethics in Government Act Amendments of 1985	99 Stat. 1324-1325

Source: Prepared by the Congressional Research Service (using the cited public laws in slip law form).

a. A provision in an appropriations act is determined to be "legislative" by a ruling of the chair or a vote of the chamber, upon the raising of a point of order or appeal. The provisions listed in this table, therefore, should be regarded only as "possibly legislative" in nature; although they meet criteria long used by the House and Senate to determine whether a provision is legislative, no ruling was made by the chair or the chamber in these cases. The listing is intended merely to be illustrative; it does not represent a comprehensive or systematic survey and should not be used to assess or infer any trends in House and Senate practices.

Table 4. Examples of Legislative Provisions Dropped From Omnibus Appropriations Acts

Fiscal Year	Appropriations Act	Legislative Provisiona	Commentaryb
1996	Omnibus Consolidated Rescissions and Appropriations Act of 1996 (P.L. 104-134; April 26, 1996)	Modification of timber salvage policy	Originated in Senate; dropped in conference (CQA, 1996, p. 10-14)
		District of Columbia school voucher plan	Originated in House; dropped in conference CQA, 1996, p. 10-11 and 12)
		Restriction on	Originated in House;

		Medic-aid paym-ents for abortion	dropped in conference (CQA, 1996, p. 10-16)

Table 4. (Continued)

Fiscal Year	Appropriations Act	Legislative Provisiona	Commentaryb
1997	Omnibus Consolid-ated Appropriations Act, 1997 (P.L. 104-208; September 30, 1996)	Abortion restrict-tions on overseas family planning funds (Mexico City policy)	Originated in House; dropped in conference (CQA, 1996, p. 10-52)
		Collection by states of taxes from Indian tribal businesses	Originated in House; dropped in conference (CQA, 1996, p. 10-58)
		General Accounting Office review of Fo-rest Service's mana-gement plan for the Tongass National Forest	Originated in Senate; dropped in conference (CQA, 1996, p. 10-58)
		Ban against most federal benefits to illegal immigrants	Originated in House; dropped in conference (CQA, 1996, p. 10-66)
		Bar against Medicare, Medicaid, and Social Security administrative funds being used to sup-port union activities	Originated in House; dropped in conference (CQA, 1996, p. 10-66)
		Exemption for cer-tain workplaces from a safety regul-ation requiring employees to wear long pants	Originated in House; dropped in conference (CQA, 1996, p. 10-66)
1999	Omnibus Consolidated and Emergency Supplemental Appropriations Act, 1999 (P.L. 105-277; October 21, 1998)	Bar against homo-sexual couples adopting children	Originated in House; dropped in conference (CQM, 10/20/98, p. 2)
		District of Colum-bia school voucher plan	Originated in House; dropped in conference (CQM, 10/20/98, p. 2)
		Parental notification regarding the prov-ision of contracep-tives to minors	Dropped in conference (CQM, 10/14/98, p. 3)
		Term limits for	Originated in House;

		high-level staff of the Federal Election Commission	dropped in conference (CQM, 10/8/98, p. 7)

Table 4. (Continued)

Fiscal Year	Appropriations Act	Legislative Provisiona	Commentaryb
		Extension of tax credit for alternative fuels	Originated in Senate; dropped in conference (CQM, 10/16/98, p. 4)

Sources: Congressional Quarterly, *CQ Almanac* (1996 and 1997) and *CQ Daily Monitor* (1998).

Notes: *CQM* refers to *CQ Monitor*; *CQA* refers to *CQ Almanac*.

a. A provision in an appropriations act is determined to be "legislative" by a ruling of the chair or a vote of the chamber, upon the raising of a point of order or appeal. The provisions listed in this table, therefore, should be regarded only as "possibly legislative" in nature; although they meet criteria long used by the House and Senate to determine whether a provision is legislative, no ruling was made by the chair or the chamber in these cases. The listing is intended merely to be illustrative; it does not represent a comprehensive or systematic survey and should not be used to assess or infer any trends in House and Senate practices.

b. In the case of the three omnibus appropriations acts listed in this table, all of the legislative provisions were dropped in conference; however, such provisions sometimes are dropped at earlier stages of the legislative process. Whether the provision originated in the House or the Senate is indicated. In this context, origination in a chamber means that it was offered in the markup of the Appropriations Committee or subcommittee of that chamber, was offered during floor consideration by that chamber, or was proposed in conference by the conferees of that chamber.

c. The three omnibus appropriations acts incorporated the full text of several of the regular appropriations acts. Legislative provisions listed under these omnibus acts may have been dropped in the conference on the omnibus act or beforehand in a conference on one of the regular appropriations acts subsequently incorporated into the omnibus act.

End Notes

[1] Legislative provisions in annual appropriations acts often are referred to colloquially as "riders." In many instances, the term "riders" is intended by some to apply also to "limitation provisions" (i.e., provisions that bar the use of appropriations for certain specified purposes) in such acts. Whereas legislative provisions usually deal with matters extraneous to the issue of funding and usually are out of order under House and Senate rules, limitation provisions are an integral part of funding issues and usually do not violate

the rules. The use of the term "riders" is avoided in this report because it is slang and because there is no common agreement as to whether it should apply to limitation provisions as well as legislative provisions.

[2] From the late 1960s through 2004, the House and Senate Appropriations Committees had 13 parallel subcommittees that each reported one of the regular appropriations acts. The two Appropriations Committees revised their subcommittee structure in 2005, at the beginning of the 109th Congress, reducing the number of subcommittees to 10 in the House Appropriations Committee and 12 in the Senate Appropriations Committee. The subcommittee structure was revised again in 2007, at the beginning of the 1 10th Congress, resulting in 12 parallel subcommittees in the House and Senate Appropriations Committees.

[3] Under the recodification of the House rules on January 6, 1999 (pursuant to the adoption of H.Res. 5, this provision was moved to Clause 4 from Clause 5(a).

[4] See the consideration in the Congressional Record of March 16, 1995, of an amendment offered by Senator Kay Bailey Hutchison to H.R. 889, a supplemental appropriations and rescission act.

[5] The measure simply declared the following: "Resolved, That the presiding officer of the Senate should apply all precedents of the Senate under rule 16, in effect at the conclusion of the 103rd Congress."

[6] See Section 903 of H.R. 566, the Miscellaneous Appropriations Act for FY2001, as enacted into law by cross- reference in P.L. 106-554 (114 Stat. 2763A-198; December 21, 2000).

[7] For more information on omnibus appropriations acts, see CRS Report RL32473, *Omnibus Appropriations Acts: Overview of Recent Practices*, by Robert Keith.

[8] The Senate's "deeming resolution" was included as Section 14007 in the Defense Appropriations Act for FY2005 (P.L. 108-287; August 5, 2004). For additional information on this topic, see CRS Report RL3 1443, *The "Deeming Resolution": A Budget Enforcement Tool*, by Robert Keith.

In: Overview of Congressional Appropriations   ISBN: 978-1-61209-849-4
Editors: J.M. Stewart, D.M. Allworth   © 2011 Nova Science Publishers, Inc.

Chapter 8

SUPPLEMENTAL APPROPRIATIONS: TRENDS AND BUDGETARY IMPACTS SINCE 1981

Thomas L. Hungerford

SUMMARY

Hurricane Katrina, which struck Louisiana, Mississippi, and Alabama in 2005, caused widespread flooding, significant property damage, and lost lives. Within two weeks, Congress passed two supplemental appropriations measures providing a combined $62.3 billion for relief and recovery needs. Including the supplementals for the war on terror and military operations in Iraq and Afghanistan, total supplemental appropriations for FY2005 to FY2008 were $512.7 billion. In response, there is growing sentiment in Congress that military operations be funded through the regular appropriations process rather than through supplemental appropriations.

Supplemental appropriations provide additional funding to an agency during the course of a fiscal year for programs and activities that are considered too urgent to wait until next year's budget. The major purposes of supplemental appropriations have changed over the past 28 years. In the 1980s, almost half of supplemental appropriations were for mandatory programs such as unemployment compensation, and the rest were for discretionary spending. After 1990, over 90% of supplemental appropriations have been for discretionary spending, as the major purpose has shifted toward funding natural disaster relief and, more recently, military operations.

The amount of new budget authority contained in supplemental appropriations bills fell after 1981 from over 3% of total budget authority to only about 0.1% by 1988. Except for a sharp spike in 1991 to fund the first Gulf war, supplemental appropriations remained at less than 1% of total budget authority throughout most of the 1990s. Supplemental appropriations began to rise after 1998, and by 2005 reached about 6% of budget authority.

Since FY1981, an average of 32% of the supplemental appropriations were offset by rescissions. After FY2002, however, about 5% of the supplemental appropriations were offset through rescissions. It has been argued, however, that the offsetting rescissions were merely write-offs of budget authority that would never be used. For example, CBO estimated that in the 1980s, nearly half of the rescinded funds were unlikely to ever have been spent.

Supplemental appropriations net of rescissions have usually increased the budget deficit, and federal debt held by the public is larger than it would have been had the supplemental appropriations been fully offset. Had supplemental appropriations been fully offset since 1981, federal debt held by the public could have been reduced by about 23% or $1,332 billion. This could have reduced interest payments to the public by $57 billion per year. On the other hand, if 25% of the supplemental appropriations in FY2003 through FY2008 had been offset (the average offset for previous years), federal debt held by the public would have been reduced by almost 3% or about $170 billion. Presently, reducing federal debt held by the public by $170 billion could save over $7 billion annually in interest payments to the public. This report may be updated if events warrant.

INTRODUCTION

Hurricane Katrina, which struck Louisiana, Mississippi, and Alabama in 2005, caused widespread flooding, significant property damage, and lost lives. Within two weeks, Congress passed two supplemental appropriation measures providing a combined $62.3 billion for relief and recovery needs. Including the supplementals for the war on terror and military operations in Iraq and Afghanistan, total supplemental appropriations were $160.4 billion for FY2005, $93.4 billion for FY2006, $120.0 billion for FY2007, and $138.7 billion for FY2008—6.3%, 4.5%, 4.2%, and 4.4% of the total budget authority, respectively.[1] In response, there is growing sentiment in Congress that military operations be funded through the regular appropriations process rather than through supplemental appropriations.[2] Supplemental appropriations often receive less scrutiny than the budget for the upcoming fiscal year as is reflected by the fact that the time from introduction to enactment is typically quite short. For example, for the five FY2005 supplemental appropriations acts, the time from introduction to enactment varied from less than one day to three months.[3]

A supplemental appropriation is a device to provide additional funds for a fiscal year already underway, and has been used since the second session of the first Congress. However, concern has been expressed over the volume of appropriations made through supplementals. Although supplemental appropriations are usually used to fund emergency spending, Congress has nevertheless attempted to control supplementals. Besides efforts to limit supplemental appropriations to "dire" emergencies, Congress has tried to mitigate the effects of supplementals with offsetting rescissions. Since 2003, however, about 5% of supplemental appropriations have been offset.

Many in Congress have expressed concern about the impact of supplemental appropriations on the federal budget deficit and federal debt. In 2001, the federal budget ran a surplus equal to 1.3% of gross domestic product (GDP). Three years later, the federal budget was in deficit as outlays increased somewhat and receipts fell. The budget deficit was equal to 3.6% of GDP in 2004 and the 2008 budget deficit was about 3.2% of GDP ($455 billion). Furthermore, federal debt held by the public as a percentage of GDP increased from 33% to about 37% between 2001 and 2008.[4]

This report examines supplemental appropriations since 1981. The trends in, and the budget rules and laws applicable to, supplemental appropriations are briefly reviewed. In addition, the impact of supplemental appropriations on budget deficits and federal debt is estimated. The report does not focus on the reasons why supplemental appropriations have followed a particular trend (although some reasons are offered), but rather focuses on the budgetary impacts of supplemental appropriations.

BUDGET RULES AND SUPPLEMENTAL APPROPRIATIONS

Supplemental appropriations provide additional funding to an agency during the course of a fiscal year for programs and activities that are considered too urgent to wait until next year's budget. They often include spending for items authorized after the annual regular appropriations process. Over the past 25 years, Congress and the President have enacted one to eight supplemental appropriations or rescissions each year.

The major purposes of supplemental appropriations have changed over the past 25 years. In the 1980s, almost half of supplemental appropriations were for mandatory programs such as unemployment compensation, and the rest was for discretionary spending. One large discretionary item in supplemental appropriation during this time was civilian pay raises. The purposes of supplemental appropriations shifted dramatically in the 1990s toward funding natural disaster relief as agencies were required to absorb the full amounts of pay raises.[5] After 1990, over 90% of supplemental appropriations were for discretionary spending.

The President is authorized to "submit to Congress proposed deficiency and supplemental appropriations the President decides are necessary because of laws enacted after submission of the budget or that are in the public interest."[6] Supplemental appropriations, however, are generally discouraged. For example, the Office of Management and Budget (OMB) directs agencies to "make every effort to postpone actions that require supplemental appropriations."[7] OMB further states that it "will only consider requests for supplementals and amendments when:

- Existing law requires payments within the fiscal year (e.g., pensions and entitlements);
- An unforeseen emergency situation occurs (e.g., natural disaster requiring expenditures for the preservation of life or property);
- New legislation enacted after the submission of the annual budget requires additional funds within the fiscal year;
- Increased workload is uncontrollable except by statutory change; or
- Liability accrues under the law and it is in the Government's interest to liquidate the liability as soon as possible (e.g., claims on which interest is payable).[8]

Supplemental appropriation bills often contain funding requests for several purposes with varying levels of urgency. For example, the Emergency Supplemental Appropriations Act for Defense, the Global War on Terror, and Tsunami Relief, 2005 (P.L. 109-13) provided $76.2 billion for additional defense spending, $5.8 billion for additional non-defense spending and $1.5 billion in rescissions which permanently cancel budget authority. Included in the bill were emergency supplemental appropriations for the National Oceanic and Atmospheric Administration, the Public Health and Social Services Emergency fund, and the Office of Federal Housing Enterprise Oversight, among others.

Supplemental and regular appropriations have been subject to a variety of budgetary rules over the years.[9] Prior to 2003, the Budget Enforcement Act of 1990 (BEA) set discretionary spending caps and a pay-as-you-go (PAYGO) requirement for mandatory spending. The BEA was revised and extended throughout the 1990s and the limits expired at the end of FY2002. Before 1990, the Balanced Budget and Emergency Deficit Control Act of 1985 set a deficit target and established a sequestration process to enforce the targets.[10] In addition, the 1987 and 1989 budget summits focused on reducing the deficit by limiting the amounts Congress could appropriate.

Spending determined to be for an emergency by both the President and Congress has been effectively exempt from the deficit targets, budget caps, and PAYGO requirements. However, at one point in the negotiations during the 1989 budget summit, negotiators discussed limiting supplemental appropriations by requiring all additional discretionary spending be offset. Unable to reach agreement on new language, the final agreement left intact the exemption for supplemental appropriations in the case of emergencies from the 1987 Budget Summit.[11] Many times the emergency designation has proven controversial, and some lawmakers have been concerned that the emergency spending exemption has been used mainly to evade BEA's constraints rather than respond to unanticipated needs.[12]

GENERAL TREND IN SUPPLEMENTAL APPROPRIATIONS

Since 1981, supplemental appropriations have varied from $1.3 billion to $161.9 billion which corresponds to 0.1% to over 6% of total budget authority (see the solid line in **Figure 1**).[13] The amount of new budget authority contained in supplemental appropriations bills fell after 1981 from over 3% of total budget authority to 0.1% in 1988. The early 1980s were characterized by high inflation and then a severe recession. The double digit inflation of 1980 and 1981 led the Federal Reserve Board to adopt a tight monetary policy to reduce inflation. This policy action contributed to the severe 1981-1982 recession. Both the high inflation and the recession led to greater than expected outlays as the price increases made programs more expensive to administer and the recession increased outlays for unemployment compensation and means-tested transfers to the unemployed. Some of the unexpected spending was funded through supplemental appropriations. As the economy recovered after 1982, the need to meet unanticipated outlays was removed, and supplemental appropriations fell. CBO argued that provisions in the Congressional Budget Act of 1974 also contributed to the reduction in supplemental appropriations in the late 1970s and early 1980s.[14]

The brief decline in 1988 may have been due to the 1987 budget summit between Congress and the President where it was agreed that supplemental appropriations would not be considered except for dire emergencies. Except for a sharp spike in 1991 to fund the first Gulf war, supplemental appropriations remained at less than 1% of total budget authority throughout most of the 1990s. Much of the incremental cost for the first Gulf War operations was eventually offset over the 1990s by burden-sharing contributions from allied nations.

After 1998, supplemental appropriations began to rise as the federal budget began running surpluses. After 2002, much of the supplemental appropriations was for funding the wars in Iraq and Afghanistan, and the war on terrorism. By 2005, supplemental appropriations reached about 6% of budget authority. Supplemental appropriations were $139.0 billion in 2008 (about 4% of budget authority) of which $305 million was offset through rescissions.

BUDGET CONTROLS AND RESCISSIONS

The enactment of rescissions, to some extent, reduced the budgetary effect of supplemental appropriations. The dashed line in Figure 1 shows the supplemental appropriations net of rescissions as a percentage of budget authority. The level of rescissions in supplemental appropriations has varied from year to year, with particularly large rescissions in FY1981, FY1986, and FY1995. In FY1995, enacted rescissions totaled $18.9 billion, while supplemental appropriations amounted to $6.4 billion. Since FY1981, an average of 33% of the supplemental appropriations were offset by rescissions. If the three years with large rescissions are omitted, then about 19% of the supplemental appropriations have been offset, on average.

Deficit reduction has been of great concern since the early 1980s. The large deficits of the early 1980s prompted Congress to enact deficit target legislation in 1985. In 1990, the focus shifted from budget deficits, per se, to establishing discretionary spending limits and mandatory spending PAYGO requirements. These limits expired at the end of FY2002. **Table 1** reports supplemental appropriations and rescissions for the following four periods:

- FY1981-FY1985, the period before the enactment of the deficit targets, but covered by provisions of the Congressional Budget Act of 1974 which required the President's budget submission to include allowances for emergencies;
- FY1986-FY1990, the period covered by the deficit targets under the Balanced Budget and Emergency Deficit Control Act of 1985, and the 1987 and 1989 budget summit agreements;

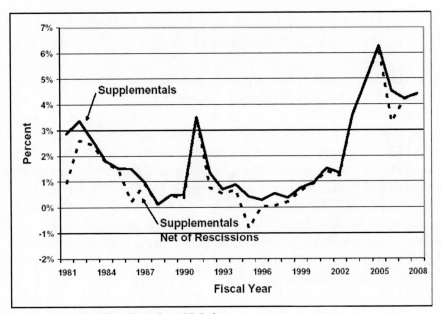

Source: CRS calculations based on CBO data.

Figure 1. Supplemental Appropriations as a Percentage of Budget Authority, 1981-2008.

- FY1991-FY2002, the period covered by BEA's discretionary limits and PAYGO requirements; and
- FY2003-FY2008, the period after the BEA limits expired.

For each of the four periods, **Table 1** shows the total amount of supplemental appropriations and rescissions. For the FY1981-FY1985 period,

22% (25% in present value terms) of supplemental appropriations were offset through rescissions.[15] Over the period covered by the deficit targets (FY1986-FY1990), over 40% of the supplemental appropriations were offset. During the FY1991-FY2002 period, about one quarter of the supplemental appropriations were offset. After FY2002, however, about 5% of the supplemental appropriations were offset through rescissions of which $34.8 billion occurred in FY2006 (about 92% of total rescissions since FY2003). It has been argued that the offsetting rescissions were merely write-offs of budget authority that would never be used. For example, CBO estimates that in the 1980s, nearly half of the rescinded funds were unlikely to ever have been spent.[16]

BUDGETARY IMPACTS OF SUPPLEMENTAL APPROPRIATIONS

Table 2 reports the estimated percentage increase in the budget deficit as a result of not offsetting the full amount of supplemental appropriations.17 Over the entire FY1981-FY2007 period, the annual budget deficits were about 12% larger than would have been the case if the entire supplemental appropriation were offset by budget reductions or revenue increases. Over the FY1981-FY1985 period, supplemental appropriations net of rescissions increased the budget deficit by about 8% per year. Over the FY1986-FY1990 period, the supplementals increased the annual budget deficits by less than 4%. After the expiration of the discretionary limits and PAYGO requirements at the end of FY2002, supplemental appropriations net of rescissions increased the budget deficit by almost 40% per year.

Supplemental appropriations have been fully offset in only one year since FY1980. In FY1995, supplemental appropriations amounted to $6.4 billion while the new Congress rescinded about $18 billion in budget authority. Consequently, supplemental appropriations net of rescissions have usually increased the budget deficit and federal debt held by the public is larger than it would have been had the supplemental appropriations been fully offset. Had supplemental appropriations been fully offset since 1981, federal debt held by the public could have been reduced by about 23% or $1,332 billion. This could have reduced interest payments to the public by $57 billion per year. On the other hand, if 25% of the supplemental appropriations in FY2003 through FY2008 had been offset (the average offset for previous years), federal debt held by the public would have been reduced by almost 3% or almost $169 billion. Presently, reducing federal debt held by the public by $169 billion could save over $7 billion annually in interest payments to the public.

Table 1. Supplemental Appropriations and Rescissions (Billions of Dollars)

Fiscal Years	Total Supplemental Appropriations	Total Rescissions	Percent of Supplemental Appropriation Rescinded(nominal)	Percent of Supplemental Appropriation Rescinded (present value)
1981- 1985	$103.3	$23.2	22.4%	25.5%
1986- 1990	$38.6	$15.7	40.7%	43.5%
1991- 2002	$206.6	$55.2	26.7%	27.0%
2003- 2008	$749.2	$37.7	5.0%	4.9%

Source: CRS calculations based on CBO and OMB data.

Table 2. Effect of Supplemental Appropriations Net of Rescissions on Budget Deficit

Fiscal Years	Estimated average annual increase in budget deficit or decrease in budget surplus
1981-1985	7.6%
1986-1990	3.5%
1991-2002	5.3%
2003-2008	36.8%
1981-2008	12.1%

CONCLUSIONS

Reacting to disasters and other emergencies often requires high levels of funding. The required funding cannot be anticipated and the length of the funding commitment is difficult to determine in advance. In adopting budget rules and laws to control supplemental appropriations, Congress and the President have in the past provided a "safety valve" for emergencies. Spending that is deemed an emergency was effectively exempt from discretionary limits and PAYGO requirements. However, what constitutes an emergency has not been without controversy.[18]

Funding for most emergencies has come through supplemental appropriations. While most of the funds from a supplemental appropriation are directed toward addressing the stated emergency, funding for other purposes with varying levels of urgency are often included. Prior to 2003, varying amounts of supplemental appropriations were offset by reductions in other spending or increases in revenues. Between 1981 and 2002, about a quarter of supplemental appropriations were offset through rescissions. However, since the expiration at the end of FY2002 of the discretionary limits and PAYGO requirements, about 5% of supplemental appropriations have been offset.

Even with the rescissions, supplemental appropriations have generally increased the budget deficit and federal debt held by the public. Had all supplemental appropriations since 1981 been offset, publicly held federal debt could have been about 23% lower at the end of FY2008. Furthermore, if just 25% of supplemental appropriations in FY2003-FY2008 had been offset, federal debt held by the public could have been almost 3% lower.

End Notes

[1] See Congressional Budget Office, CBO data on Supplemental Budget Authority for the 2000s, at http://www.cbo.gov/ ftpdocs/66xx/doc6630/SuppApprop.pdf, visited Dec. 29, 2008.
[2] See CRS Report RS22455, *Military Operations: Precedents for Funding Contingency Operations in Regular or in Supplemental Appropriations Bills*, by Stephen.
[3] The Emergency Supplemental Appropriations Act to Meet Immediate Needs Arising from the Consequences of Hurricane Katrina, 2005 (P.L. 109-61) was introduced and enacted on Sept. 2, 2005. The Military Construction Appropriations and Emergency Hurricane Supplemental Appropriations Act, 2005 (P.L. 108-324) was introduced on July 15, 2004, and enacted on Oct. 13, 2004.
[4] At the end of 2008, total outstanding federal debt was $10.55 trillion, of which $6.32 trillion was held by the public and the balance was held in government accounts. Debt held by the public is the debt measure used in the report because it is the measure that is relevant in an economic sense. It is federal debt that is sold in credit markets, and influences the interest rate and private-sector investment decisions. See CRS Report RL31590, *The Federal Government Debt: Its Size and Economic Significance*, by Brian W. Cashell.
[5] Congressional Budget Office, *Supplemental Appropriations in the 1990s*, Mar. 2001.
[6] 31 U.S.C. §1107.
[7] Office of Management and Budget, Circular A-11 (June 2008), p. 1 of section 110.
[8] Circular A-11 (June 2008), p. 1 of section 110.
[9] See CRS Report 98-721, *Introduction to the Federal Budget Process*, by Robert Keith; and CRS Report RS21035, *Emergency Spending: Statutory and Congressional Rules*, by James V. Saturno.

[10] Sequestrations are automatic, largely across-the-board spending reductions to bring projected budget levels in line with statutory targets. See CRS Report RS20398, *Budget Sequesters: A Brief Review*, by Robert Keith.

[11] William G. Dauster, "Budget Emergencies," *Journal of Legislation*, vol. 18, no. 2, (1992), pp. 249-315.

[12] Congressional Budget Office, *Emergency Spending under the Budget Enforcement Act*, Dec. 1998.

[13] Budget authority provides the federal government authority to enter into obligations. Outlays or the spending of the money occurs when obligations are liquidated. New budget authority in one year may not result in outlays in the same year. For example, of the $2,770 billion that the administration proposed for FY2007 outlays, $2,206 billion would result from recommended new budget authority and $564 billion would result from budget authority enacted in prior years. See *Budget of the United States Government, Fiscal Year 2006, Analytical Perspectives*, Feb. 2006, chart 26-1, p. 389.

[14] Congressional Budget Office, *Supplemental Appropriations in the 1980s*, Feb. 1990.

[15] The level of supplemental appropriations and rescissions varies from year to year. The present value calculation takes into account inflation and the time value of money using the interest rate on five-year U.S. government bonds.

[16] Congressional Budget Office, *Supplemental Appropriations in the 1980s*, Feb. 1990.

[17] Supplemental appropriations may not necessarily result in outlays in the same fiscal year in which they are enacted. Based on CBO data for the 1990s, it is estimated that about 30.5% of supplemental appropriations resulted in outlays in the same fiscal year, 56.1% in the next fiscal year, and the remaining 13.4% in subsequent fiscal years. These percentages are used for estimating the impact of the outlays associated with supplemental appropriations on the budget deficit. To the extent that the rescissions just cancelled budget authority that never would have been spent, the estimates could understate the actual impact on budget deficits.

[18] See CRS Report RL31478, *Federal Budget Process Reform: Analysis of Five Reform Issues*, by James V. Saturno and Bill Heniff Jr., and Congressional Budget Office, *Emergency Spending under the Budget Enforcement Act*, Dec. 1998 for a discussion on budgeting for emergencies and a review of reform options.

In: Overview of Congressional Appropriations   ISBN: 978-1-61209-849-4
Editors: J.M. Stewart, D.M. Allworth   © 2011 Nova Science Publishers, Inc.

Chapter 9

STATE, FOREIGN OPERATIONS APPROPRIATIONS: A GUIDE TO COMPONENT ACCOUNTS

Curt Tarnoff and Kennon H. Nakamura

SUMMARY

The State, Foreign Operations, and Related Programs appropriations legislation provides annual funding for almost all of the international affairs programs generally considered as part of the 150 International Affairs Budget Function (the major exception being food assistance). In recent years, the legislation has also served as a vehicle for Congress to place conditions on the expenditure of those funds, and express its views regarding certain foreign policy issues.

This report briefly discusses the legislation generally and then provides a short description of the various funding accounts as they appear in Division H, "Department of State, Foreign Operations, and Related Programs Appropriations Act, 2009," of the Omnibus Appropriations Act, 2009 (P.L. 111-8).

INTRODUCTION

The Department of State, Foreign Operations, and Related Programs (State, Foreign Operations) appropriations bill provides annual appropriations for the vast majority of international affairs programs generally considered as part of the 150 International Affairs Budget Function.[1] The State Department portion makes up about one-third of the funding, and the Foreign Operations portion—often called the "foreign aid" bill—makes up the remainder of the funds appropriated.[2]

Among the areas covered by the State, Foreign Operations appropriations legislation, and explained below, are the Department of State and the U.S. Agency for International Development's (USAID) operating accounts, both assessed and voluntary U.S. contributions to international organizations and peacekeeping operations, U.S. non-military international broadcasting, bilateral and multilateral U.S. foreign economic assistance, assistance to foreign militaries, anti-narcotics funding, and funding for the Peace Corps, the Millennium Challenge Corporation, and the many other programs operated primarily by the Department of State and USAID through which the United States engages with the world to protect and advance U.S. national interests. Beyond providing funds, the appropriations bills, in recent years, also have been an important vehicle in conditioning the use of these funds and stating congressional views regarding foreign policy issues.

There are, however, several funding areas that are not covered by the State, Foreign Operations appropriations legislation that might be considered international affairs activities. These programs would include P.L. 480 and other food assistance, included in the 150 account but funded by the Agriculture appropriations bill. While the State Department and USAID sponsor nearly four-fifths of U.S. and foreign participants in educational and cultural exchange programs, other government agencies are responsible for the remaining participants in such programs, including, for example, the short-term exchange of scientists program at the National Cancer Institute. The Department of Defense's Commander's Emergency Response Program (CERP) supports reconstruction needs in Iraq and Afghanistan and its "Section 1206" authority supports the strengthening of foreign military capacities. These other-agency programs are funded through their own agency appropriations measures.

While the appropriation of funds is an authority reserved for the Congress by the Constitution, the two-step authorization/appropriations process is established by House and Senate rules; and the authorization of appropriations is intended to provide guidance to appropriators as to a general amount and under what conditions funding might be provided to an agency or program.[3] However, in the case of the State Department and foreign assistance programs, it is prescribed by law that legislation authorizing appropriations is required before the appropriations can be made.[4] These provisions have been waived in the years that Congress has not enacted authorizations.[5]

Within the appropriations legislation, account names have changed over the years and new accounts have been added. In FY2008, for example, the International Disaster and Famine Assistance account became the International Disaster Assistance account. In the FY2009 bill, the Former Soviet Union account was combined with the Eastern Europe and Baltic States account to form a new Europe, Eurasia, and Central Asia account. In the FY2006 bill, a new Democracy Fund was established. The overall organization of the legislation may change as well. The FY2009 bill added a new title (Title II), specifically for USAID operations.

In the FY2009 Omnibus Appropriations Act (P.L. 111-8), the State Department, Foreign Operations, and Related Programs appropriations legislation (Division H) is divided into seven titles:

Title I	Department of State and Related Agencies
Title II	United States Agency for International Development
Title III	Bilateral Economic Assistance
Title IV	International Security Assistance
Title V	Multilateral Assistance
Title VI	Export and Investment Assistance
Title VII	General Provisions

This report briefly explains the different accounts in the order they are presented in the FY2009 State, Foreign Operations appropriations legislation.

ACCOUNT DESCRIPTIONS

TITLE I—DEPARTMENT OF STATE AND RELATED AGENCIES

Title I provides funds for (1) the personnel, operations, and programs of the Department of State; (2) U.S. participation in international organizations, such as the United Nations as well as small commissions such as the International Boundary and Water Commission between the United States and Mexico; (3) U.S. government, non-military-international broadcasting; and (4) several U.S. non-governmental agencies whose purposes also help promote U.S. interests abroad, and other U.S. commissions and interparliamentary groups more directly related to U.S. foreign policy initiatives such as the U.S. Commission on International Religious Freedom.

Administration of Foreign Affairs

The Administration of Foreign Affairs account category provides for the personnel, operations, and programs of the Department of State as well as the construction and maintenance of its facilities around the world.

Diplomatic and Consular Programs (D&CP)
Diplomatic and Consular Programs is the operating account of the Department of State. It includes salaries for all its employees; funding for the operations of the Office of the Secretary, the deputy secretaries, and the under secretaries; funding for the operations of the various regional, functional, and administrative bureaus and their programs associated with the conduct of foreign policy; "non-bricks-and-mortar" security including funds for a guard force, armored vehicles, security training, and electronic and other technical security systems; telecommunications; medical care; transportation and travel; and training.

Civilian Stabilization Initiatives (CSI)
CSI seeks to improve and maintain an U.S. civilian capability to assist fragile and failed states that are coming out of crisis and conflict situations to stabilize and rebuild the country and its society. While the George W. Bush Administration requested funding for the Civilian Stabilization Initiatives to be fully under the Department of State, Congress divided funding of CSI through both the State Department and USAID. Working in the State Department, the Coordinator for Reconstruction and Stabilization (S/CRS), is to coordinate the U.S. government interagency response. Along with the funds identified for USAID to provide for the USAID's component to the Civilian Stabilization Initiative, S/CRS is to recruit, organize, train, equip, and deploy if necessary a three-layer Civilian Response Corp—the Active Response Corps, and the

Standby Response Corps from 17 federal agencies and the Department of Defense, and the larger Civilian Reserve Corps from the private sector.

Capital Investment Fund (CIF)

The Capital Investment Fund was created in 1994 to provide for purchasing information technology and other capital equipment to ensure efficient management, coordination, and communications.

Office of the Inspector General (OIG)

This account funds the State Department's Office of the Inspector General, which conducts independent audits, inspections, and investigations of the programs and offices of Department of State and the Broadcasting Board of Governors (BBG).

Educational and Cultural Exchange Programs

With funds appropriated to this account, the State Department manages U.S. educational exchanges, such as the Fulbright and Humphrey Fellowships, and citizen exchanges, such as the International Visitors Leadership Program, and the Sports United and Youth Exchange programs that focus on middle and high school students. Cultural exchange programs include sending the *Neo Classic Blues Duo* to Ghana and Togo to perform and discuss blues melodies from the 1920s and 1930s and sending the Harlem Gospel Choir to perform in Lebanon.

Representation Allowances

Funding for the Representation Allowances account provides partial reimbursement to Ambassadors, Principal Officers, and some Foreign Service for costs associated with maintaining vital contacts in the host country where they are assigned.

Protection of Foreign Missions and Officials

The U.S. Diplomatic Security Service permanently or intermittently protects international organizations and foreign missions and officials in New York City and elsewhere in the United States.

Embassy Security, Construction, and Maintenance (ESCM)

The Embassy Security, Construction and Maintenance account is divided in two parts: (1) Ongoing Operations, which funds the general maintenance and support of U.S. State Department facilities both in the United States and abroad, and (2) Worldwide Security (WWS) Upgrades, which funds the construction and security upgrades of embassy and facilities around the world.

Emergencies in the Diplomatic and Consular Services

The Emergencies account addresses unexpected events, such as the evacuation of U.S. diplomats and their families from an embassy, medical evacuations, and travel expenses related to natural disasters. This account also pays for rewards for information related to international terrorism, narcotics-related activities, and war crimes tribunals.

Buying Power Maintenance Account

The Buying Power Maintenance account helps the Department of State manage exchange rate losses in the cost of its overseas operations.

Repatriation Loan Program

The Repatriation Loan Program allows the U.S. government to provide funds, on a loan basis, to U.S. citizens abroad who become destitute and are unable to fund their return to the United States.

Payment to the American Institute in Taiwan (AIT)

The American Institute in Taiwan acts as an unofficial U.S. consulate. The account supports a contract providing for salaries, benefits, and other expenses associated with maintaining the Institute.

Foreign Service Retirement and Disability Fund

The Fund is a mandatory expense that covers the U.S. government's portion of maintaining the retirement program for the Foreign Service and Foreign Service Nationals/Locally Hired Employees. Contributions to this fund are made by both the employee and the hiring agency.

International Organizations

Through the two accounts in the International Organizations category, the United States meets its assessed obligations to the many international organizations and peacekeeping efforts that the United States supports.

Contributions to International Organizations (CIO)

The International Organizations account under the Department of State funds the assessed U.S. contributions to the United Nations (U.N.) and U.N. system organizations, Inter-American organizations, and various regional organizations to which the United States belongs through U.S. law, treaty, or convention. U.S. contributions to organizations funded through the CIO account generally provide about 25% of each organization's budget.

Contributions for International Peacekeeping (CIPA)

The International Peacekeeping account funds assessments on the United States for the 16 current U.N. Peacekeeping operations around the world and two ongoing War Crimes Tribunals regarding Yugoslavia and Rwanda. U.S. contributions generally provide about 27% of the various organizations' budgets.

International Commissions

Accounts under the International Commissions category were established by treaties and agreements that the President ratified with the advice and consent of the Senate. The accounts provide funding for the U.S. portion of the salaries and programs of the following bilateral and multilateral commissions:

- International Boundary and Water Commission between the United States and Mexico,
- International Fisheries Commissions,
- Border Environment Cooperation Commission,
- International Joint Commission (between the U.S. and Canada), and
- International Boundary Commission (between the U.S. and Canada).

Broadcasting Board of Governors (BBG)

The nine-member Broadcasting Board of Governors supervises and funds all non-military, U.S. government international broadcasting. Operating in 60 languages, these broadcasts include Voice of America (VOA), Broadcasting to Cuba (Radio and TV Marti), Radio Free Europe/Radio Liberty (RFE/RL), Radio Free Asia (RFA), and the Middle East Broadcasting Network (MBN), which includes Alhurra, Alhurra-Iraq, Alhurra-Europe, and Radio Sawa. The broadcasting category is generally divided into the following two accounts:

International Broadcasting Operations

The Operations account funds the operations of the BBG and all U.S. government, non-military international broadcasts, including salaries and benefits of management, administrative staff, broadcasters, and reporters; contracts with surrogate broadcasters such as Radio Free Asia; provision of office and broadcasting studio facilities; transitioning to new communications methods such as greater use of the Internet; and other operating expenses.

Broadcasting Capital Improvements

The Capital Improvements account supports maintenance of the BBG from broadcast station repair to the building of new antennas.

Related Programs

Under this category, funds are provided to several non-governmental organizations that have objectives that are similar to views and positions advocated by the United States in its foreign policy. These non-governmental organizations provide educational programs, exchanges, and grants to organizations in foreign countries promoting democracy, rule of law, economic development, open markets, literacy, women's rights, and many similar objectives. Most of these organizations are nonprofit organizations and receive funding from both the U.S. government, through appropriated funds, and through private donations.

The Asia Foundation

The Foundation seeks to strengthen democratic processes and institutions in Asia, open markets, and improve U.S.-Asian relations.

United States Institute of Peace (USIP)

The U.S. Institute of Peace mission is to promote international peace through educational programs, conferences, and workshops, professional training, applied research, and dialogue facilitation in the United States and abroad.

International Center for Middle Eastern-Western Dialogue

The Center convenes policy discussion meetings, and develops programs of cooperative study for those working on issues related to the growth of civil society and democratic institutions, and the peaceful resolution of differences among the countries of the Middle East and between the countries of the Middle East and Western nations.

Eisenhower Exchange Fellowship Program

The Exchange Program brings professionals who are rising leaders in their countries to the United States and sends their U.S. counterparts abroad with a custom-designed program for each participant to make contacts and learn about the other's country and work environment.

Israeli-Arab Scholarship Program (IASP)

The IASP funds scholarships for Israeli Arabs to attend institutions of higher education in the United States.

The Center for Cultural and Technical Interchange Between East and West (East-West Center)

The East-West Center promotes understanding and cooperation among the governments and peoples of the Asia/Pacific region and the United States.

National Endowment for Democracy (NED)

NED is a private, non-profit organization established to support democratic institutions in over 90 countries.

Other Commissions

The Commissions and groups in the Other Commissions category of the State, Foreign Operations legislation, are organizations that are established by an Act of Congress to advance certain U.S. objectives in the international arena. In the Federal Budget submission to the Congress, these organizations are listed under the legislative Branch Boards and Commissions, but are funded through the State, Foreign Operations legislation. The funding meets the operational and programmatic requirements of these organizations.

Commission for the Preservation of America's Heritage Abroad

The Commission seeks to purchase, restore, or preserve endangered cultural sites in Eastern and Central Europe important to the heritage of U.S. citizens, and seeks help from other governments in this effort.

Commission on International Religious Freedom (CIRF)

In consultation with the State Department, the Commission seeks to promote international religious freedom.

Commission on Security and Cooperation in Europe (CSCE)

The Commission oversees the work of the Organization on Security and Cooperation in Europe (OSCE), particularly in the area of humanitarian affairs.

Congressional-Executive Commission on the People's Republic of China

The Commission monitors China's compliance with international human rights agreements and standards.

United States-China Economic and Security Review Commission

The Commission monitors, investigates, and submits to Congress an annual report and recommendations on the national security implications of the bilateral trade and economic relationship between the United States and the People's Republic of China.

United States Senate-China, United States Senate-Russia Interparliamentary Groups

This account supports the participation of U.S. Senators in the United States Senate-China Interparliamentary Group and the United States Senate-Russia Interparliamentary Group.

TITLE II—UNITED STATES AGENCY FOR INTERNATIONAL DEVELOPMENT (USAID)

This title provides operational funds for USAID, an independent agency directly responsible for most bilateral development assistance and disaster relief programs, many of which are funded in Title III.

U.S. Agency for International Development Operating Expenses (OE)

The Operating Expense account funds the operational costs of USAID including salaries and benefits, overseas and Washington operations, human capital initiatives, security, and information technology maintenance and upgrades.

Civilian Stabilization Initiative

The Civilian Stabilization Initiative, a portion of which is also funded under the Department of State Title I, here supports the hiring and training of USAID personnel and prepositioning of equipment for the standby response corps, the rapid "surge" element of any deployment to address emergency stabilization needs.

Capital Investment Fund

A program begun in FY2003, the Capital Investment Fund supports USAID construction of facilities overseas, with an emphasis on improving security and enhancing information technology.

USAID Office of Inspector General

This account supports operational costs of USAID's Inspector General office, which conducts audits and investigations of USAID programs.

TITLE III—BILATERAL ECONOMIC ASSISTANCE

Under this title, funds are appropriated in support of U.S. government departments and independent agencies conducting humanitarian, development, and other programs meeting U.S. foreign policy objectives throughout the world.

Funds Appropriated to the President

Funds in this category of appropriations are provided chiefly through USAID or in close association with the Department of State.

Global Health and Child Survival (GHCS)
The Global Health and Child Survival account supports multiple health programs conducted by USAID and the Department of State through funding of two major elements:

Child Survival and Health Programs (CSH)
Managed by USAID, appropriations in the CSH sub-account fund programs focused on combating infectious diseases such as HIV/AIDS; malaria; tuberculosis; maternal and child health; vulnerable children; and family planning and reproductive health.

Global HIV/AIDS Initiative (GHAI)
Managed by the Office of the Global AIDS Coordinator (OGAC) in the Department of State, the Global HIV/AIDS Initiative sub-account is the largest source of funding for the President's Emergency Plan for AIDS Relief (PEPFAR). The account also supports part of the U.S. contribution to the multilateral organization, the Global Fund to Fight AIDS, Tuberculosis and Malaria.

Development Assistance (DA Account)
Managed by USAID, the Development Assistance account funds programs in agriculture, private sector development, microcredit, water and sanitation, education, environment, democracy and governance, among others.

International Disaster Assistance (IDA)
Managed by the USAID Office of Foreign Disaster Assistance, the account aids nations struck by natural and manmade disasters and emergencies. It was previously referred to as the International Disaster and Famine Assistance account (IDFA).

Transition Initiatives
The Transition Initiatives account supports the activities of USAID's Office of Transition Initiatives (OTI), a program launched in 1994 to bridge

the gap between disaster and development aid. It supports flexible, short-term assistance projects in transition countries that are moving from war to peace, civil conflict to national reconciliation, or where political instability has not yet erupted into violence and where conflict mitigation might prevent the outbreak of such violence.

Development Credit Authority (DCA)

Managed by USAID, the Development Credit Authority provides for the administrative costs of several USAID credit programs, including loan guarantees that allow private banks to finance housing shelter projects, water and sanitation systems, and microcredit and small enterprise development programs.

Economic Support Fund (ESF)

The Economic Support Fund uses economic assistance to advance U.S. strategic goals in countries of special importance to U.S. foreign policy. Funding decisions are made by the State Department; programs are managed by both USAID and the State Department.

Democracy Fund

The Fund supports democratization programs run by the State Department's Bureau of Democracy, Human Rights and Labor (DRL), and USAID's Office of Democracy and Governance.

International Fund for Ireland

This activity supports the Anglo-Irish Accord and efforts to spur economic and commercial development in Northern Ireland.

Assistance for Europe, Eurasia, and Central Asia

This new account combines two formerly separate accounts into one. The two accounts were:

Assistance for Eastern Europe and the Baltic States

This account is commonly known as the SEED Act account (Support for East European Democracy), its authorizing legislation (P.L. 101-179). Since 1989, USAID, under the guidance of the State Department, channeled most U.S. economic assistance to Eastern Europe through this regional program.

Assistance for the Independent States of the former Soviet Union

This account is commonly known as the FREEDOM Support Act account (Freedom for Russia and Emerging Eurasian Democracies and Open Markets Support Act), its authorizing legislation (P.L. 102-511). Through this regional program, launched in 1992, USAID and multiple other agencies, under the guidance of the State Department, extended economic aid to the 12 countries of the former Soviet Union.

Department of State

International Narcotics Control and Law Enforcement (INCLE)

The INCLE account funds international counternarcotics activities; anti-crime programs, including trafficking in women and children; and rule of law activities, including support for judicial reform. The INCLE account includes funds to support the U.S.-Mexico Mérida Initiative to enhance bilateral and regional cooperation to combat drug trafficking and organized crime.

Andean Counterdrug Initiative (ACI)

The Andean Counterdrug Initiative, created in FY2000 as the Plan Colombia account, supports a multi-year counternarcotics effort in the Andean region, providing assistance for both drug interdiction and alternative development.

Nonproliferation, Anti-terrorism, Demining, and Related programs (NADR)

This account funds a variety of State Department-managed activities aimed at countering weapons proliferation and terrorism and promoting demining operations in developing nations.

Migration and Refugee Assistance (MRA)

The Migration and Refugee Assistance program supports refugee relief activities worldwide and, in some cases, helps resettle refugees.

Emergency Refugee and Migration Assistance (ERMA) Fund

ERMA holds funds that can be drawn upon quickly in times of refugee emergencies. Appropriations replenish resources to this account.

Independent Agencies

Peace Corps

The Peace Corps sends U.S. volunteers to developing countries to provide technical aid and to promote mutual understanding on a people-to-people basis.

Millennium Challenge Corporation (MCC)

Established in 2004, the MCC supports large-scale, multi-year development projects designed and implemented by recipient countries, which are selected on the basis of their commitments to good governance, investment in health and education, and support for economic freedom.

Inter-American Foundation (IAF)

The IAF, an independent agency, finances small-scale enterprise and grassroots self-help activities aimed at helping poor people in Latin America.

African Development Foundation (ADF)

The ADF, an independent agency, finances small-scale enterprise and grassroots self-help activities aimed at helping poor people in Africa.

Department of the Treasury

International Affairs Technical Assistance

This technical assistance program supports financial advisors to countries seeking help in implementing economic reforms and improving financial management of government resources. In addition, funds have been used to address terrorist financing activities.

Debt Restructuring

This account provides funds to reduce, and in some cases forgive, debts owed to the U.S. by poor countries, especially those in Africa and the small economies in Latin America and the Caribbean. In recent years, funds have supported the U.S. commitment to the Heavily Indebted Poor Country (HIPC) Initiative.

TITLE IV — INTERNATIONAL SECURITY ASSISTANCE

Funds Appropriated to the President

Peacekeeping Operations (PKO)

Unlike the Title I Contributions to Peacekeeping Activities (CIPA) account, which provides assessed funds for peacekeeping forces, the PKO account provides voluntary support for multilateral efforts in conflict resolution, including the training of African peacekeepers and funding operations of the Multinational and Observers Mission in the Sinai.

International Military Education and Training (IMET)

Through IMET, the United States provides military training to selected foreign military and civilian personnel. The State Department and the Department of Defense share policy authority, and the Department of Defense implements this program.

Foreign Military Financing (FMF) Program

The Foreign Military Financing Program supports U.S. overseas arms transfers on a grant basis. The State Department and the Department of Defense share policy authority, and the Department of Defense implements this program.

TITLE V — MULTILATERAL ECONOMIC ASSISTANCE

Funds Appropriated to the President

Under this category, funds are provided through the Department of State to international organizations, including the United Nations.

International Organizations and Programs (IO&P)

This account provides voluntary donations to support the programs of international agencies involved in a range of development, humanitarian, and scientific activities, including the U.N. Development Program (UNDP), U.N. Environment Program (UNEP), U.N. Children's Fund (UNICEF), and U.N. Population Fund (UNFPA).

International Financial Institutions

Under this category, funds are provided through the Department of the Treasury to a wide range of multilateral financial institutions, which offer loans—both "soft" (i.e., concessional) and "hard" (i.e., near-market rate)—and some grants to developing countries and private sector entities in those countries. Not all international financial institutions require or receive U.S. contributions from year to year.[6]

Global Environment Facility (GEF)
Cosponsored by the UNDP, UNEP, and the World Bank, the GEF makes grants to help developing countries deal with global environmental problems.

World Bank: International Development Association (IDA)
As the World Bank's "soft loan" window, IDA lends at concessional rates to low-income countries. The International Bank for Reconstruction and Development (IBRD) is the World Bank window that provides loans on near-market terms to promote economic development primarily in middle-income countries, based largely on bond sales. Another World Bank window, the International Finance Corporation (IFC), makes loans and equity investments to promote growth of productive private enterprise in developing nations.

Enterprise for the Americas Multilateral Investment Fund (MIF)
The MIF is a multi-donor trust fund providing technical and financial assistance to help countries in Latin America and the Caribbean reform their investment policies in order to attract foreign investment. It resides within the Inter-American Development Bank, which promotes economic and social development in Latin America and the Caribbean by providing near-market rate loans through its ordinary capital account and concessional loans to the poorest nations through its Fund for Special Operations (FSO). The Inter-American Investment Corporation (IIC), makes loans and equity investments to promote the growth of private enterprise.

Asian Development Fund (ADF)
The ADF is the "soft loan" window of the Asian Development Bank (ADB), which finances economic development programs in Asia and the Pacific.

African Development Fund (AfDF)

The African Development Fund (AfDF) lends on concessional terms to low-income sub-Saharan African countries. It resides within the African Development Bank (AfDB), which lends at near- market rates, with special emphasis on agriculture, infrastructure and industrial development.

International Fund for Agricultural Development (IFAD)

IFAD is a multilateral financial institution helping developing countries increase agricultural productivity and income, improve nutritional levels, and integrate into larger markets.

TITLE VI—EXPORT AND INVESTMENT ASSISTANCE

Export-Import Bank

The Export-Import Bank issues loan guarantees and insurance to commercial banks that make trade credits available to American exporters. The Bank also extends direct loans to U.S. businesses, especially those whose counterparts abroad receive foreign government-subsidized trade credits.

Overseas Private Investment Corporation (OPIC)

OPIC offers political risk insurance, guarantees, and investment financing to encourage U.S. firms to invest in developing countries.

Trade and Development Agency (TDA)

The TDA finances feasibility studies and other project-planning services for major development activities in developing countries, to support economic development and to promote U.S. exports.

TITLE VII— GENERAL PROVISIONS

Under the General Provisions title are limitations and prohibitions on assistance, notification and reporting requirements, and more detailed funding mandates for specific accounts in other titles of the legislation.

End Notes

[1] International Affairs is one category of the various components of the federal budget designated by the Office of Management and Budget (OMB). Each category represents a major objective and operation of the Federal Government. Each function and sub-function is assigned a three digit code. International affairs is 150. Subfunction 151 encompasses International development and humanitarian assistance. Accounts under the International Commissions category of the legislation are the exception—they are part of the 300 Natural Resources Budget Function.

[2] Until the 110th Congress, the State Department and Foreign Operations portions of the bill were developed in different Appropriations subcommittees and considered as separate bills.

[3] CRS Report RS20371, *Overview of the Authorization-Appropriations Process*, by Bill Heniff Jr.

[4] See sec. 15 of the State Department Basic Authorities Act of 1956 (22 U.S.C. 2680) and sec. 10 of the Foreign Military Sales Act amendments, 1971 (22 U.S.C. 2412).

[5] For example, see sec. 7023 of the FY2009 Omnibus Appropriations Act, Division H (P.L. 111-8). Most foreign operations program appropriations have not been authorized since 1985.

[6] Among those that sometimes receive funding but for which there was no request or appropriation in FY2009 are:

World Bank Multilateral Investment Guaranty Agency (MIGA). MIGA encourages private investment in developing countries by offering insurance against noncommercial risks such as expropriation.

European Bank for Reconstruction and Development (EBRD). The EBRD lends at near-market rates to help East European and former Soviet states adopt market economies. Private sector and privatizing public sector firms receive substantial amounts of EBRD lending.

North American Development Bank (NADBank). The NADBank is governed by the United States and Mexico as part of the North American Free Trade Agreement (NAFTA). It began lending in 1996 to finance environmental infrastructure projects along the U.S./Mexico border, as well as community adjustment and investment activities in both nations.

CHAPTER SOURCES

Chapter 1 - This is an edited, reformatted and augmented version of a Congressional Research Service publication, 97-684, dated December 2, 2010.

Chapter 2 - This is an edited, reformatted and augmented version of a Congressional Research Service publication, RS20441, dated November 22, 2010.

Chapter 3 - This is an edited, reformatted and augmented version of a Congressional Research Service publication, RL32473, dated August 25, 2010.

Chapter 4 - This is an edited, reformatted and augmented version of a Congressional Research Service publication, RL34597, dated August 25, 2010.

Chapter 5 - This is an edited, reformatted and augmented version of a Congressional Research Service publication, RL31055, dated November 19, 2010.

Chapter 6 - This is an edited, reformatted and augmented version of a Congressional Research Service publication, R40083, dated May 18, 2009.

Chapter 7 - This is an edited, reformatted and augmented version of a Congressional Research Service publication, RL30619, dated December 4, 2009.

Chapter 8 - This is an edited, reformatted and augmented version of a Congressional Research Service publication, RL33134, dated January 2, 2009.

Chapter 9 - This is an edited, reformatted and augmented version of a Congressional Research Service publication, R40482, dated March 30, 2009.

INDEX

A

Abraham, 112
adjustment, 153
Afghanistan, ix, 15, 92, 123, 124, 128, 136
Africa, 149
agencies, viii, 2, 3, 4, 7, 12, 15, 25, 26, 91,
    92, 95, 96, 99, 100, 101, 126, 136, 138,
    139, 145, 148, 150
agriculture, 5, 22, 146, 152
AIDS, 146
Air Force, 106
Alaska, 105, 112
American Recovery and Reinvestment Act,
    98
American Recovery and Reinvestment Act
    of 2009, 98
Asia, 141, 142, 143, 151
assets, 53
audits, 139, 145

B

background information, vii, 37, 38, 93
ban, 99
BEA, 39, 127, 129
benefits, 119, 140, 142, 145
bonds, 133
Budget Committee, 77, 83
budget deficit, 124, 125, 128, 130, 132, 133

budget resolution, 2, 5, 6, 18, 19, 20, 21, 22,
    23, 24, 29, 31, 32, 34, 35, 39, 46, 77, 78,
    93, 108
budget surplus, 131
businesses, 119, 152

C

capital account, 151
Caribbean, 149, 151
cash, 4, 31, 91
Census, 80
Central Asia, 137, 147
Central Europe, 144
children, 119, 146, 148
China, 47, 112, 144
citizens, 140
City, 111, 119, 139
civil society, 143
Civilian Stabilization Initiative, 138, 145
Colombia, 148
commercial, 147, 152
commercial bank, 152
community, 153
compensation, 35, 97, 123, 126, 128
compliance, 32, 144
concessional terms, 152
conditioning, 136
conference, 10, 11, 12, 19, 21, 22, 25, 26, 27,
    29, 30, 31, 32, 42, 71, 86, 87, 92, 93, 101,
    108, 109, 118, 119, 120
Conference Report, 30

conflict, 138, 147, 150
conflict resolution, 150
congressional budget, 8, 9, 35, 44
Congressional Budget Act of 1974, 39, 128, 129
Congressional Budget Office, 21, 31, 34, 35, 82, 95, 98, 132, 133
consent, 8, 9, 27, 30, 76, 81, 89, 92, 93, 103, 141
Consolidated Appropriations Act, 41, 46, 47, 49, 50, 52, 64, 65, 67, 68, 70, 106, 107, 108, 110, 111, 113, 114, 116
Constitution, 2, 11, 28, 30, 57, 73, 92, 136
construction, 4, 82, 138, 140, 145
contingency, 25, 35
controversial, 89, 127
controversies, viii, 99, 100, 104
convention, 141
cooperation, 143
coordination, 139
cost, 24, 128, 140
covering, viii, 37, 39, 40, 44, 51, 55, 56, 58, 59
credit market, 132
CSCE, 144
Cuba, 141

D

DCA, 147
debts, 149
deficiency, 126
deficit, 35, 125, 127, 128, 129, 130, 131
Delta, 113, 117
democracy, 142, 146
Democratic Party, 57
democratization, 147
Department of Defense, 25, 28, 53, 58, 136, 139, 150
Department of Homeland Security, 58
Department of Labor, 85
developing countries, 149, 151, 152, 153
developing nations, 148, 151
development assistance, 144
dichotomy, 47, 102

disaster, 144, 147
disaster relief, 144
diseases, 146
disposition, 7, 92
distribution, 12, 19, 82
District of Columbia, 40, 42, 43, 52, 64, 65, 68, 70, 110, 112, 117
donations, 97, 142, 150
draft, 29
drug trafficking, 148

E

earnings, 31
Eastern Europe, 137, 147
economic assistance, 136, 147
economic development, 142, 151, 152
economic reform, 149
economic reforms, 149
economic relations, 144
education, vii, 1, 2, 146, 149
educational exchanges, 139
educational programs, 142
election, 56, 57, 58, 64, 66, 72
eligibility criteria, 31
embassy, 140
emergency, 24, 25, 32, 39, 83, 93, 125, 126, 127, 132, 145
employees, 2, 96, 119, 138
enforcement, 20, 23, 33, 34, 46, 52, 108
environment, 146
equipment, 139, 145
equity, 151
Eurasia, 137, 147
Europe, 137, 141, 144, 147
evacuation, 140
exchange rate, 140
executive branch, 87, 96
expenditures, viii, 4, 35, 91, 95, 96, 126
exporters, 152
exports, 152

F

failed states, 138
families, 140
family planning, 119, 146
FDA, 117
federal funds, 35
federal government, viii, 2, 4, 31, 52, 58, 77, 91, 99, 100, 133
Federal Government, 132, 153
federal law, 4, 35, 91
Federal Reserve Board, 127
Filipino, 112
financial, 4, 35, 91, 149, 151, 152
financial institutions, 151
flexibility, 87, 108
flooding, viii, 123, 124
food, ix, 135, 136
force, 27, 138
Ford, 13, 16
foreign aid, 136
foreign assistance, 137
foreign investment, 151
foreign policy, ix, 135, 136, 138, 142, 145, 147
formula, 15, 40, 101
freedom, 144, 149
FREEDOM Support Act, 148

G

GAO, 93
GDP, 125
General Accounting Office, 96, 119
governance, 146, 149
government funds, 4
grants, 142, 151
grassroots, 149
gross domestic product, 125
growth, 143, 151
guidance, 137, 147, 148
guidelines, 100
guiding principles, 87
Gulf Coast, 111

Gulf of Mexico, 28
Gulf war, 124, 128

H

health, 104, 146, 149
Health and Human Services, 3, 14, 21, 46, 85
HHS, 42, 46, 64, 68
high school, 139
higher education, 143
HIPC, 149
hiring, 140, 145
history, 52
HIV, 146
HIV/AIDS, 146
Hmong, 110
homeland security, vii, 1, 2
Homeland Security Act, 47, 112
host, 139
119, 120, 121, 136
House Manual, 92, 93, 94
House of Representatives, 6, 14, 17, 30, 51, 92, 95, 98
housing, 147
Housing and Urban Development, 3, 14, 21, 30, 42
HUD, 38, 40, 41, 49, 64, 67, 107, 112
human, 144, 145
human capital, 145
human right, 144
human rights, 144
Hurricane Katrina, viii, 123, 124, 132

I

IASP, 143
immigrants, 119
impeachment, 58, 64
in transition, 147
income, 31, 151, 152
Independence, 113
individuals, 91
inflation, 127, 133

informal negotiations, 30
information technology, 139, 145
infrastructure, 152, 153
injury, iv
inspections, 139
institutions, 142, 143
intelligence, 28, 58
Inter-American Development Bank, 110, 151
international affairs, ix, 135, 136
International Bank for Reconstruction and Development, 151
International Development Association (IDA), 151
international financial institutions, 151
International Financial Institutions, 151
International Narcotics Control, 148
international terrorism, 140
investment, 132, 149, 151, 152, 153
investments, 151
Iraq, ix, 15, 92, 105, 123, 124, 128, 136, 142
Ireland, 147
issues, viii, ix, 13, 37, 38, 43, 120, 135, 136, 143, 152

J

Jamestown, 114
jurisdiction, 1, 3, 5, 7, 8, 9, 11, 18, 19, 25, 26, 27, 28, 29, 31, 77, 92
justification, 5

K

Kids in Disasters Well-being, Safety, and Health Act of 2007, 47, 110

L

languages, 141
Latin America, 149, 151
laws, 2, 37, 39, 106, 118, 125, 126, 131
leadership, 96, 104

Lebanon, 139
legislative proposals, 58
lending, 153
LIFE, 113
liquidate, 126
literacy, 142
loan guarantees, 147, 152
loans, 31, 151, 152
Louisiana, viii, 123, 124

M

majority, 6, 7, 15, 23, 24, 43, 88, 136
malaria, 146
management, 46, 139, 142, 149
mark up, 7
materials, 5
matter, iv, 9, 10, 87, 101, 103, 104
measurements, 39
Medicaid, 105, 114, 119
medical, 138, 140
medical care, 138
Medicare, 31, 52, 112, 114, 119
Mexico, 119, 138, 141, 148, 153
Middle East, 141, 143
military, ix, 123, 124, 136, 138, 141, 142, 150
minimum wage, 104
minors, 119
mission, 142
missions, 139
modifications, 39
monetary policy, 127
Montana, 115

N

narcotics, 136, 140
National Institutes of Health, 85
national interests, 136
national security, 144
NATO, 116
natural disaster, 123, 126, 140
natural disasters, 140

nonprofit organizations, 142
North America, 153
North American Free Trade Agreement (NAFTA), 153
Northern Ireland, 147

O

Obama, 13, 14, 17, 31
Office of Management and Budget, 34, 35, 46, 126, 132, 153
Office of the Inspector General, 139
officials, 7, 139
Oklahoma, 111
Omnibus Appropriations Act,, 14, 41, 50, 66, 107, 109, 135, 153
open markets, 142
operations, vii, viii, ix, 1, 2, 4, 25, 52, 61, 95, 97, 123, 124, 128, 136, 137, 138, 140, 141, 142, 145, 148, 150, 153
opportunities, 43, 76, 88, 89
organ, 100
organize, 138
OSCE, 144
Overseas Private Investment Corporation, 152
oversight, 12

P

Pacific, 143, 151
Pandemic Influenza Act, 28
parallel, 3, 120
parliamentary procedure, 80
participants, 57, 136
peace, 136, 140, 142, 147, 150
peacekeepers, 150
peacekeeping, 136, 140, 150
peacekeeping forces, 150
Persian Gulf, 115
Persian Gulf War, 115
policy, 86, 89, 100, 107, 118, 119, 127, 143, 150
political instability, 147

precedent, 99, 101
precedents, 8, 9, 25, 32, 84, 93, 121
preparation, iv, 96
present value, 130, 131, 133
preservation, 126
presidency, 13, 31, 58
president, 98
President, vii, 3, 4, 5, 7, 11, 13, 15, 21, 28, 29, 31, 37, 38, 39, 44, 45, 46, 58, 64, 66, 67, 96, 97, 98, 107, 126, 127, 128, 129, 131, 141, 146, 150
Presidential Administration, 13, 14, 16, 17
Privacy Protection Act, 115
private banks, 147
private investment, 153
professionals, 143
profit, 143
project, 4, 10, 12, 79, 84, 152
proliferation, 148
proposition, 88
protection, 89
public debt, 1, 58
public interest, 126
public sector, 153

R

reading, 81, 92
recession, 127
recommendations, iv, 7, 28, 144
reconciliation, 147
reconstruction, 136
recovery, ix, 123, 124
reform, 133, 148, 151
Reform, 110, 111, 115, 116, 117, 133
refugees, 148
regional cooperation, 148
relief, ix, 123, 124, 126, 148
Reorganization Act, 116
repair, 142
reporters, 142
Republican Party, 57
requirements, 8, 9, 10, 12, 19, 24, 45, 53, 81, 127, 129, 130, 132, 143, 153

resolution, 2, 5, 6, 15, 17, 18, 20, 23, 24, 30, 32, 35, 38, 39, 40, 43, 59, 61, 62, 63, 64, 66, 67, 71, 77, 96, 100, 108, 121, 143
resources, 148, 149
response, ix, 5, 28, 34, 123, 124, 138, 145
restrictions, 47, 84, 86, 90, 100, 103
retirement, 140
revenue, 39, 130
rewards, 140
risk, 152
risks, 153
Romania, 117
rule of law, 142, 148
rules, vii, viii, 1, 2, 5, 8, 9, 10, 18, 22, 23, 26, 27, 29, 30, 31, 32, 46, 47, 76, 77, 81, 83, 87, 88, 89, 90, 92, 93, 99, 100, 102, 103, 120, 121, 125, 127, 131, 136
Russia, 144, 148
Rwanda, 141

S

safety, 119, 131
sanctions, 3
savings, 44, 45, 46
school, 118, 119
scope, 9
security, 138, 140, 145
shelter, 147
signs, 97
Sinai, 150
social development, 151
Social Security, 19, 31, 52, 119
society, 138
soft loan, 151
South Dakota, 115
Soviet Union, 137, 148
stabilization, 145
Standing Rules, 31
state, 35, 92, 103
states, 2, 73, 119, 126, 153
statutory authority, 12, 87
structure, 52, 78, 121
sub-Saharan Africa, 152
Sun, 111

Supreme Court, 113
surplus, 125

T

Taiwan, 140
target, 5, 127, 128
tax incentive, 104
taxes, 115, 119
technical assistance, 149
telecommunications, 138
Tennessee Valley Authority, 110
terrorism, 128, 148
time constraints, 38
time periods, 13
Title I, 95, 98, 111, 137, 144, 145, 150
Title II, 96, 98, 137, 144, 145
Title IV, 111, 137, 150
Title V, 85, 137, 150, 152, 153
Togo, 139
trade, 13, 144, 152
trade-off, 13
trafficking, 148
training, 138, 142, 145, 150
transformation, 42, 43
transportation, 5, 138
Treasury, 2, 4, 14, 64, 68, 91, 149, 151
treaties, 141
trust fund, 97, 151
Trust Fund, 97
tuberculosis, 146

U

uniform, 45
United, 51, 103, 106, 110, 112, 118, 133, 136, 137, 138, 139, 140, 141, 142, 143, 144, 150, 153
United Nations, 138, 141, 150
United States, 51, 103, 106, 110, 112, 118, 133, 136, 137, 138, 139, 140, 141, 142, 143, 144, 150, 153

V

vacancies, 10, 24
valve, 131
vehicles, 47, 104, 138
veto, 3, 11, 46
Vietnam, 113
violence, 147
vote, 3, 6, 10, 11, 23, 24, 32, 88, 101, 103,
    106, 108, 118, 120
voting, 10

W

waiver, 9, 24, 32, 89
war, ix, 123, 124, 128, 140, 147
war crimes, 140

War on Terror, 126
Washington, 14, 17, 19, 21, 92, 93, 118, 145
water, 146, 147
weapons, 148
wear, 119
White House, 13
work environment, 143
Workforce Investment Act, 110
workload, 126
World Bank, 105, 151, 153
worldwide, 148

Y

yield, 45
Yugoslavia, 141